Thank you for your support. Best Wishes in the New Year!

Ron _____

Praise for Romi Hancock and
She Believed She Could & She Did

Exposing every part of her life, the author lays out a road map to transform your life by being who you really are. With a loving approach, she reveals how to embrace the courage to be vulnerable and acknowledge the fear that can stand in the way of success. In a nutshell, it's a bold call to fail. get up, and try again.

— Susan Friedmann, CSP, international bestselling author of *Riches in Niches: How to Make it BIG in a Small Market*

If you want to have an incredible experience, get into Romi's world. I've done work with Romi in different instances and each time my life is better for it. She has an enormous heart, a knack for helping her clients accelerate results and her tenacity and commitment to making a difference is unheralded. If you have a chance to be around and learn from Romi, take it. You'll be happy you did.

— Setema Gail, Author, Coach, Founder of Shield Maiden

Romi Hancock has written a must-read guide for anyone holding back from embracing personal success by overcoming fears. Not your typical self-help book. Authentic storytelling weaved with self-inquiry journaling provides thoughtful ways for discovering your true power within.

— Cynthia Luvlee, CEO Shyne San Diego

Romi Hancock's book will transform your thoughts and bring you into a new level of love and understanding. There are many women who spend a lifetime seeking inner strength to move forward. The author of this book is a woman of love, perseverance, and inspiration. It takes tremendous courage to revisit the pain that others have placed upon you, but it takes a warrior to share how to overcome it.

— Shuree Wesley, CEO M&S Wesley, Entrepreneur

If you want to experience, achieve and realize your biggest dreams goals and visions in life, then start here! This booked is jam packed with strategies, techniques and ideas proven to help you turn your most far reaching goals into your closest reality.

— Patrick Snow, Publishing Coach and International Best-Selling Author of *Creating Your Own Destiny*

Romi's book is beautifully written with her personal soft transparency and honesty, forgiveness, and grace. It breathes hope to a broken world where children are too often used as innocent pawns for the selfish needs of others, only to grow up and repeat the patterns themselves. Romi was that child, but refused to allow the generational cycle to continue, and her book is the roadmap for others to rise up and succeed. I've healed and grown from reading it, and I know that everyone who reads it will be blessed with the same.

— Russ Womack, Author of *Orange*

Romi's bravery, steadfast determination and willingness to share her life's story will bring light to solutions that can end sex trafficking. No one should have to endure the horrifying events that took place in Romi's life. Thank God Romi was able to get out and create an amazing and powerful life for her and her family. If you have the opportunity to read Romi's book and go through her life coaching program your life will truly be enhanced. I have been blessed to be able to call her my friend, my Sister.

— Onyx Jones, Author, CFO Culver City

Romi continues to challenge herself mentally and physically to be her best self. There have been times in our lives where she has pushed me and reminded me to get up and put one foot forward. She has always been my cheerleader and reminds me to stop and celebrate our successes. Romi is my friend, sister and mentor.

— Kathleen Stephens, Financial Advisor

SHE BELIEVED SHE COULD & SHE DID

FROM SURVIVORSHIP TO LEADERSHIP: A ROADMAP TO SUCCESS

ROMI HANCOCK

AVIVA PUBLISHING
New York

SHE BELIEVED SHE COULD & SHE DID
From Survivorship to Leadership: A Roadmap to Success

Copyright © 2019 by Romi Hancock All rights reserved.

Published by:
Aviva Publishing
Lake Placid, NY, USA
(515) 523-1320
www.AvivaPubs.com

All Rights Reserved. No part of this book may be used or reproduced in any manner whatsoever without the expressed written permission of the author. Address all inquiries to:

Romi Hancock
Email: romi@romihancock.com
Website: www.romihancock.com

ISBN (hardcover): 978-1-947937-75-8
Library of Congress Control Number: 2019905521

Editor: Russ womack
Cover Design and Interior Book Layout: Nicole Gabriel, Angel Dog Productions

Every attempt has been made to source properly all quotes.

Printed in the United States of America

I dedicate this book to my husband, Viktor, for his unwavering support, and my amazing kids, Dominique, Andre, Catalina, Maggie, and Ella. This book would not have been possible without them. I love you all!

ACKNOWLEDGEMENTS

I'd like to thank the following people who have been a part of my life and the unfolding of it. God strategically placed them in my life at the perfect time: Lisa Lamont, Tony Robbins, Patrick Snow, Josh Warnock, Dr. Wayne Dyer, Mano Agulian, Russ Womack, Marko Lipozencic, Keno Clarke, Setema Gali, Robert Villanueva, Kerry Smith

FOREWORD

Author Romi Hancock takes us on a personal journey where many have never ventured, and most would never dare. We're witnesses to her tragic childhood filled with dysfunction, foster homes, sexual abuse, correctional facilities, and running away at 15 years old—only to be forced into the world of trafficking. We cheer her on as she escapes the horrors, and we finally exhale alongside her as she discovers a taste of normalcy, love, marriage, and children. Maybe we exhaled too early; maybe we're ignorant and callused to the weight of tragedy, and the realization that it can surely return. We cry with her as she finds herself once again scared, alone, and unsure of what the next breath looks like. When she opens her eyes she finds herself a widow with two young children. Most people will never experience such terrors and horrors in their cumulative lifetime.

Romi experienced all of them and more before her 25th birthday.

She had all the reason to give up, but she refused. The world gave her every reason to be angry, but instead she chose love. She could have become a victim, but she chose empowerment instead.

And she wrote it all down.

After reading *She Believed She Could & She Did,* I can say with absolute assurance that this book is a must read for all audiences. It levels the playing field in a world that tricks you into thinking some of us are special and entitled, and some are simply not loveable. The words contained within these pages remind us that we are actually no different from each other, but rather very much alike. There is a part of Romi somewhere inside us all—a person who has suffered far too much, standing between here and nowhere, having to make a desperate choice.

It's a comfortable place within these pages because she clothes the words with compassion and grace. She wears the words loosely for a world that is all too familiar with the tightening grip of fear and anxiety, shame, and damnation. You no longer need to bow to fear or run from that which scares you. If you're standing paralyzed at your personal crossroad unable to find the Northern Star, Romi's words will guide you. Turn to page one if you have lost hope. There's no condemnation from her words. Condemnation, shame, and guilt don't exist in the heart of a person who has been to hell and returned stronger, more loving, more graceful.

You'll feel at home when her words wrap themselves around your shattered heart, and soothe the deep scars that never seem to fade. She'll sit with you as you turn each page, never leaving your side, because the tears that fall across the hardened wrinkles chiseled from your past that seems unimaginable to others, are all too familiar to Romi. She's cried those tears, and she knows the places they come from.

Her successes and victories in life are incredible and hopeful for all of us. She chose to win, she chose victory, and became a powerful Transformation Life Coach, and one of the most successful real estate brokers in the country alongside an amazing husband and five beautiful children. She could have relaxed into this new world—if anyone had the right to do so, she did. But contentment and pride aren't found in her vocabulary. She could very well demand what the world owes her, what the world took from her, but instead she gives and she loves, because humility appears when we don't forget where we've been, and deciding to help others gives us purpose and meaning.

Her faith in God is powerful and sustaining. It's a faith that pulled her through the darkest of seasons when the thought of no longer breathing became appealing and within arm's reach. Her love for God is deep and sustaining, honest and real. It's a relationship that was built on remembering what if felt like to be locked in a closet for weeks at a time, and knowing that God never left her, and never forgot her.

It's difficult to believe when it's dark, when it's hard to remember the last time you truly smiled. It's also difficult to believe that anyone else understands.

Romi does.

She understands you, and she wants nothing more than to give you what she knows. She refuses to allow what she has suffered to be victorious. She refuses to allow tragedy to win.

Come alongside her and let her tell you her story, and let her tell you what it looks like to breakthrough victoriously. She has written a roadmap especially for you, wherever you stand today. If you've been through enough, suffered far too much, and are standing today unsure of where to take your next step, I have the answer.

Your next step is to turn the page and begin to discover, to believe, to heal.

— Russ Womack, Author of *Orange*

CONTENTS

FOREWORD	9
INTRODUCTION	15
I. LETTING GO OF WHAT DOES NOT SERVE YOU	19
II. FINDING YOUR STRENGTH	29
III. LETTING GO OF FEAR	39
IV. TAKING THE FIRST STEPS	49
V. GOING AFTER WHAT YOU WANT	57
VI. FORGIVING YOURSELF	67
VII. TRUSTING YOUR INSTINCTS	77
VIII. FINDING YOUR PURPOSE	87
IX. CHALLENGING YOURSELF	95
X. ATTACKING ANXIETY	105
XI. FAILING IS GREAT	115
XII. DESIRING MORE OUT OF LIFE	123
XIII. USING THE KNOWLEDGE AROUND YOU	133
XIV. INVEST IN YOURSELF	141
XV. ACT AS IF YOU'VE ALREADY MADE IT	151
XVI. LOVING THOSE WHO LOVE YOU	161
XVII. BECOMING A WARRIOR	169
XVIII. CREATE A ROADMAP AND FOLLOW THE STEPS	177
CONCLUSION	185
PRINCIPLES TO PURSING AND CREATING PASSION, WEALTH, AND HEALTH	187

INTRODUCTION

My life has been constantly shaken by unexpected challenges, big and small, without any respite or a moment to breathe and feel safe. Every morning I awoke and wondered if that day would be my last. It came pretty damn close on more than one occasion, but what kept me going is that I always realized that if the situation was bad, I could handle it, and if the situation was good, it could be better. You probably have experienced similar feelings during your life and have faced those crossroads at some point as well. Maybe you're standing there today. We all have these feelings at times, regardless of our background, life situation, age, relationship status, health, employment, financial situation, or level of knowledge. How many times have you arrived at a turning point in your life, good or bad, and asked yourself, now what? Did you contemplate what your next steps should be? Did you find yourself disappointed by the things you hadn't accomplished? Did you have difficulties maintaining dedication and motivation to keep heading toward your goals?

These questions and many others are answered in this book—from my perspective, from my personal experiences. However, as much as this is a book about my life and my way of dealing with challenges, it is also a book for you, for your life, and your ability to create something bigger, better, and more meaningful for yourself and your life. This book is not for my benefit. It never was. I've lived through it and I still live it today, and all my lessons, tricks, secrets, and all my successes as well as my failures are written down within these pages.

So, to whom is this book addressed? It's for you. Not who you are today, but to the person who you want to become, and who you will become. I address that inner voice deep inside you—the same voice that encouraged you to open the first page of this book—the voice that holds all your great ideas and pure motivation, but is bullied by fear, the daily grind, prejudices, hatred, misery, and all other hardships of your life. This is not a fictional story. I won't address moral issues and smother you without factual context. I'm going to give you honesty. You deserve that.

This book documents my life and gives you my perspective, the lessons that I've learned, and extends to you the same help I received from very special people when I needed them the most. One of the instrumental people in my life is my mentor, Dr. Wayne Dyer, for whom I am grateful for as much a person can be. So what exactly is this book about? This book documents my story, from growing up in a dysfunctional family and my troubled youth, foster homes, correctional facilities, through the lowest pits of life a girl can find herself in; through unbelievable suffering, rape and torture, to the point of escape, through first glimpses of hope, the many ups and downs and shots at a decent life, and finally to complete devastation of being a widowed mom of two adorable kids—all before my 25th birthday.

But it doesn't end there. This is also a coming-of-age story that continues from my 25th birthday to today, with reflections on my life, my thoughts and questions, and the valuable lessons I've learned. Lessons I'm still learning. Lessons I'm passing on to you. It touches on family, love, health, and business aspects, and ties them into a single person—me. I am a Transformation Life Coach who can help you empower your mind, body, and soul. I encourage you to read my story of how I went from being a victim and a prisoner to having great success in fitness and nutrition; leaving it all behind to become a real estate badass, and then returning to my roots to tie it all together again. This book will show you the steps of how to recognize yourself as someone who is powerful, capable, and above all, beautiful. You are! You might not see yourself like that today as you're reading these words, but you will. I consciously give the roadmap to you—a roadmap that will help you shine as you are meant to.

— Romi Hancock

With everything that has happened to you, you can either feel sorry for yourself or treat what has happened as a gift. Everything is either an opportunity to grow or an obstacle to keep you from growing. You get to choose.

— Wayne W. Dyer

I. LETTING GO OF WHAT DOES NOT SERVE YOU

For most people, their real life starts at 25 years old. By that time, they're already settled, experienced, and they have experimented a bit. They've completed their education and have a rough idea whether they want to enjoy your freedom for a couple of more years, or jump right into it—start a career, a family, or both. What if I were to tell you that at the age of 24, I was already an "old soul" who had two kids with no job skills, no money saved, and that I just witnessed the death of the only person in my life who gave a damn about me. Scary, right?

Well, that's a story you might have heard before—or a version of it, and it's not like I was the only single mom at the time. I ask that you pay attention to is the "old soul" part; this part of the story is rare, because by the time I was 25, I had already experienced the amount of suffering that most people are not exposed to in an entire lifetime.

I was an unwanted child, and I knew it from an early age. I was repeatedly told, directly and indirectly, that I was unwanted and worthless. My mother was an alcoholic, the bad kind, and I was mistreated for as long as I can remember. I was a burden in her life, and she made damn sure to point that out to me. Verbal and physical abuse was my reality, and in-between her drunken stupors and sober episodes where she blamed me for all of her problems, I was left wondering *what comes next in life?* Every day was a great uncertainty and, as you can imagine, such an environment can negatively affect a little girl. By the age of 13, I had left school and was placed in a foster home. That wasn't the end of my suffering—it was the beginning. It's hard to imagine that so many bad things could happen to a person, and especially at an age where I was too young to understand why I had to endure such horrific circumstances.

The foster home was a hell hole, and I could have lived with that if only I didn't have to deal with abuse as well. My mom didn't have high living standards, but this place was a thousand times worse; it wasn't fit for an animal. You see, my foster dad wasn't an alcoholic like my mom, but I would have rather he was because then he wouldn't have had the desire to sexually abuse me. The more I refused him and struggled, the worse he became. I mustered up the courage to report him to the police knowing that I could very well end up on the streets all alone if I got kicked out of the foster home. No one believed me. I was labeled a liar and a deviant teenager that caused trouble wherever I went. Well, instead of getting kicked out onto the streets, I was sent to a juvenile detention for over a year—all because I dared to stand up for myself and make a complaint. So much for being protected by the system!

I was 13 years old and imprisoned with no one to love and protect me. I had no real friends, or friends of any kind for that matter, and all of my role models were abusive people who saw me as a ragdoll. My entire life was filled with the horrors of abuse. I was in a perpetual state of stress and uncertainty. So when I met a man who spoke to me with a kind voice and treated me with decency, I was surprised and enchanted. His name was Goldie and he would come and visit another girl in juvenile detention. I don't even think I was really attracted to him; I didn't even see him as a friend, but at that time in my life, he was someone I thought I could trust. He was the first person who gave me the confidence to believe that everything could turn out all right. We spoke often and I took his number just in case I needed help once I got out. Two days after I turned 15, I was sent to a girl's home, but the worm of doubt began to eat away at me. I experienced this before, and it didn't end well for me. I was scared that they would send me back to either my mom's, the juvenile detention, or back to the foster home. These were all horrible places and I would rank them in that order. Imagine a 15-year-old girl who would rather live in a prison than with her own mother. I had to take control of my life, even if that meant being on my own. So I ran away the first chance I got, determined never to go back to the horrors of my old life.

I called Goldie, the only person I trusted, and he came to my rescue in a shiny Cadillac and took me far away—so far that I didn't know where the heck we were when we stopped traveling. I was free for a few days; I was out—so I thought. I wasn't really out because I had no money, no real home, and no family. It was me and Goldie, who promised to help me get my life back on track. It wasn't long before I found out that his idea of helping was putting me to work. Working didn't mean sending me to clean toilets or wash the dishes in some dirty old restaurant—not even close. A week into our getaway he told me that I was to become a prostitute and give him the money I earned. Imagine the feeling of being betrayed by the first person you ever trusted, and imagine the shock of hearing those words come out of his mouth. After explaining in great detail that I was supposed to sell myself to strangers and give him the money I earned, he simply added that that was the way the world worked.

I refused.

As a result, I received a vicious beating. It was a familiar cycle repeating itself all over again. I remember thinking at the time, *what the hell did I do to deserve a life like this?*

This went on for a couple of weeks and each time I refused to obey him, I got a beating. Once he figured out I wasn't going to be his golden goose, he sold me to another pimp. They bagged me like I was a pig and drove me in the middle of the night to a new "owner". This savage owned a brothel. He had the same plan for me as Goldie, but he took it a step further. After I refused to obey his commands, he had me repeatedly beaten and raped. My life at 15 years old became a vicious cycle of beatings, rape, and abuse, and I never had the chance to do anything about it. Even with the torture, I never stopped looking for a way out. I tried escaping once, but failed, and my pimp decided that I wasn't worth the trouble and traded me to another guy. Not only did he trade me, but he warned the pimp of my disobedience and my stubbornness, and so the new guy made sure that I got treated even worse. As soon as I arrived at my new destination, I was told to do the same thing—get out into the streets and have sex with strangers and you won't get punished. I still refused to budge, but this pimp was determined to break me. He gave me beatings that almost broke every bone in my body. During this time I was powerless to do anything. There were no other people around, there was no phone, I didn't know where I was, and I was bruised and hurt.

Just think about that for a second. I thought about my life a lot at that time, and the only shred of my personality remaining was my perseverance. These savage people took everything from me: my childhood, my freedom, my innocence. They abused me in ways you could not even begin to imagine. They forced themselves on me; I was repeatedly raped and starved, and I was beaten to the point of being unrecognizable.

They were still unable to break me.

After a couple of weeks, I was chained up and stuffed in a closet like I was a dog. I was in isolation for so long that I lost track of the days, weeks, and months. He told me that he would keep me there until I did what I was told, or, I would die in there. Most of you don't know, and I hope you never find out, what solitude and isolation does to a person. Most people go crazy after a couple of days of solitary confinement. I wasn't someone convicted of a heinous crime, nor was I any sort of a beast that deserved such punishment. I was an innocent 15-year-old girl that no one was looking for. I was a runaway, which meant no one was ever going to ask questions about me, and if I died in that closet, no one would ever find out what happened to me. I was kidnapped and no one gave a damn. Imagine being chained in a dark closet for weeks with only these thoughts continually going through your mind. There wasn't a single happy moment I could remember, a single stroke of light that would keep my spirit strong; I believed that I was never going to be rescued. All the beatings in the world can't even come close to the feeling of being utterly helpless.

I finally broke.

I couldn't keep it up anymore and I finally agreed to do what he asked. He let me out of the closet, dressed me and walked me out to the street. He was standing no more than 10 feet from me as cars drove by. The days came and went and not one person stopped; I wasn't making money, and he was becoming angrier. I knew that it would be the end of me if I didn't get a client soon. A gentleman in a Cadillac pulled up and I got a sickening feeling in my stomach, because the last time I got into a Cadillac with a stranger, it didn't end well.

I had no choice.

It was my only chance, and I knew that if I didn't pull it off, I wasn't going to be alive another day. As I got into the car, I pointed to my pimp who was watching me from the street and said to the man in the car, "If you don't get me out of here, that savage is going to kill me." The guy believed me. You know why? Because he heard the truth in my words and the desperation in my eyes. He stepped on the gas and drove off. I knew better than to tell him to take me just anywhere. I wasn't going to make that mistake again. So I told him to drop me off at a public place. It was a pool hall about 20 miles from there. He didn't even come to a complete stop when I opened a door and frantically jumped out of his car, leaving the door still open.

Any girl or woman, or any person for that matter, will tell you that being alone on the streets at the age of 15 is the worst thing that could ever happen. It was the best thing that happened to me because I survived.

I survived.

That's why I considered myself an "old soul" before the age of 25. I'd been through so much that whatever new challenges life threw at me, I was certain that I could face them.

It's been over 30 years since all of this took place and I don't think about it very often anymore. This is because I refuse to be a perpetual victim. The reason why this chapter is called "Letting Go of What Does Not Serve You" is because I did let go of all the suffering I experienced, and I focused only on the fact that I survived it all. When I look back on those years, I don't envision the pain, and I don't feel it deep inside me anymore. I have in no way forgotten about it, but I look at it *differently*. It's hard to find lessons in a mindless cycle of vicious abuse, but dug deep and found them.

I was in my 20s with 2 kids and a partner that I knew was wrong for me. I didn't know what a real man even looked like, and even he treated me right, supported me, and we had 2 beautiful children together, I knew down deep that he wasn't for me. My life wasn't perfect, but it was the closest thing to a normal life I could ever dream of during the darkest hours of the Calvary that I survived. I let go of the victim mentality that was weighing me down and I looked forward to the future.

I know it's hard to imagine that a person who went through years of abuse like I did could ever be free of the influence of those events. I am not completely free because those years shaped my mind and my soul a great deal, just not in the way you would imagine. The fact that I persevered when most people would have buckled shaped me more than all the rapes and beatings that I received. The fact that I escaped on my own when most people would have lost all hope early on left a deep and permanent mark in my soul—deeper than all the rapes that I endured combined. It took me some time, but I finally realized that the inner voice that prevented me from giving up in the face of all the horror that I received was the voice of God. Some people call it intuition, divine energy, the source, etc. For me, that's God speaking through my deepest thoughts. This is the voice that everyone can find within themselves, and all you have to do is listen. I am fully aware that sometimes it's not always easy to hear it, but when you silence your mind and empty your thoughts, you can hear it loud and clear.

Chapter 1 – Exercise

1. What are you holding onto that does not serve you anymore?

    About 3 1/2 years ago, my husband was diagnosed with Alzheimers. He was 60 years old. It was heart breaking and I feel like it is a big cloud that hangs over my life.

2. Has it been difficult to move on from the past?

    Yes

3. What are you doing to heal your inner wounds?

    I go to church. For 7 years I have been going to a weekly bible study. I think it helps.

Loving people live in a loving world. Hostile people live in a hostile world. Same world.

- Wayne Dyer

II. FINDING YOUR STRENGTH

I ran as fast to the pool hall as my feeble legs could carry me. I never looked back at the Cadillac, and never got the name of the kind stranger who saved my life. Out of all people in my life, he is one of those rare souls that I will remain indebted to.

No one talked to me for hours at that place, and I was fine with it. I would have been just fine on my own that entire day. I was understandably visibly distressed after all the abuse I had been subjected to. My body was weak and dehydrated. For a good couple of hours, I did nothing but scan the room for a familiar face and stared at the entrance every few seconds. I was in a fight-or-flight mode. I envisioned and planned grabbing the nearest sharpest object that I could find and running full steam ahead at the first sign of a familiar face. A familiar face would have meant that they were after me; everyone I knew at the time had brought me nothing but pain and suffering. I was a 15-year-old girl with the mentality of a soldier ready to face the enemy and die fighting rather than get captured again.

A few people tried to engage in a conversation with me, but I don't remember any of them because I was in too much shock. They were all erased from my memory in the adrenaline haze I was experiencing. The only voice I paid attention to was a man named Charles. The only reason I acknowledged him and not the others was because he was genuinely concerned. While other people were asking me questions that I didn't have the mental energy to answer, Charles sensed my state of mind. It was as if he heard my heartbeat like it was his own. There are people in life who, regardless of the age difference, background or the situation, simply connect to your energy. It's a God-given gift that extraordinary people are blessed with and I feel incredibly grateful that such a person found me exactly when I needed him the most.

He didn't start the conversation with "hello" or "Are you ok?" He asked me why I kept watching the doors, and why I was so scared. The kind of person leaves a huge impression on a normal person never mind someone like me who has just been through such extreme torment. I wasn't able to tell him the truth, or even the abbreviated version. I don't even remember how much I told him, but I clearly remember that he was compassionate; he listened, trying to understand as much as he could; he didn't push me to tell him anything, and perhaps that was the most important thing to me at that time. In fact, Charles never pushed toward anything, ever. He told me just a bit about himself, and I didn't even ask, but it was as if he knew that I needed to hear it. He was a pool hustler and basically lived a life of a drifter, not a literal one, but sort of a life drifter. It wasn't a sad story— his life was his choice and I could sense it right away. He let me stay with him for a week, and a week turned into years. He was the only person in the world that I actually trusted, and he never betrayed that trust, even though he had plenty of opportunities to do so.

Our life together was a struggle. Nothing compared to what I survived before we met, but a struggle none the less. Although I never was in love with Charles, I loved him very much. We never got married, even though I had two kids with him before I turned 18. We never separated, either. He was fully aware that I was not in love with him, and I suspect he wasn't in love with me either, yet we stayed together for the sake of the kids and ourselves. Charles was a rolling stone for his entire life, and I was the only steady thing he ever had. He was the only steady thing in my life, too. The money was tight, and I really mean tight. He wasn't as good of a hustler as he thought, and often times, we were dead broke. We were living on the verge of being evicted all the time, and even crossed that line on a couple of occasions. I remember the worst part was just after I gave birth to our first daughter. We ended up on the streets during the freezing cold of winter in Toronto, Canada. We ran as far away from Florida as we could for the sake of making sure that I would never be forced to go back. Legally, I was a runaway, and the police could have arrested me and sent me back "home".

Despite the hardships, I felt that I was growing stronger as a person. No matter how odd it sounds, all the difficulty we endured kept strengthening my willpower and developed my character in a way that would not have been possible under normal and safe circumstances. I felt a sense of responsibility, and slowly gained the power to take control of certain aspects of my life. When the money got really tight, I became a dancer to earn a living. It was how I survived, and at the time I was proud of it. I could pay the rent, put food on the table, and feed my children. Considering the fact that I had been robbed of my own childhood, these were the things I took control of and I never felt bad about it. Without any education, no job skills, and being sexually abused, it took a great deal of courage for me the go down that road again, but I did it for my kids, for Charles, and for me.

We struggled for a couple of years, moving from place to place, drifting through life. When I turned 18, I was no longer in danger of getting arrested for being a runaway. This was the first time ever that I had actually thought ahead for more than a week in my life. That day I realized that I could legally make my own choices in life, and I felt an incredible sense of freedom and relief. I started working out and got back in shape. Even with all our financial woes, I somehow felt better about myself. We had nothing to our name but a couple of kids and a car, but I had the freedom to shape my life the way I wanted. I started envisioning a better life for ourselves, but there was one problem. I never took action.

Thinking back to that time, I had mixed feelings about not doing better, and these feelings held sway over me for weeks on end. It was not too long ago when I finally realized that no matter what mistakes I made back then; they were not failures. These were lessons that toughened me up even more. Having my type of childhood, I was forced into being an "old soul"; I was an adolescent forced to make adult decisions. It was only natural that it took some time for me to gain enough wisdom, willpower, and courage to take action, to make new sacrifices, and to try and create something more in our lives.

This was a very important part of my life, but I wasn't aware of it back then as I am now. Among all the dark and tragic struggles, I could sense that I was becoming a person that will do great things. I was determined that once I left that life, people would remember me. I would no longer be just another victim, forgotten and irrelevant.

Within 4 years I went from being a person chained in a dark room waiting for the next horror to be bestowed upon me, to a person who realized that I was the one who decided the outcome of my life. Little did I know that four years later I would face another devastating blow, and that my life would once again take an unexpected turn.

Even with all the success I've achieved so far in my life, I often contemplate about the time when I was 20 years old. I truly believe that my best accomplishment was surviving to my 20th birthday. I

II. FINDING YOUR STRENGTH

am reluctant to label my achievements after I turned 30 as success because those successes were all built on the foundations I had laid during my teenage years. I could have given up on many times since then, and although I did give up on some, my persistence and determination were deep rooted and built on a strong foundation.

I've made mistakes here and there, but just like when I was in my teens, I never gave up on the big things. My resolve, my will and my strength were tested time and time again, sometimes with a tenfold increase in suffering and despair, but I never buckled. I didn't know it at the time, but in my early 20s, I was becoming aware that I was not a weak person. I was far from where I wanted to be, but I had survived. I gained some control over my life, but I knew that I had a long way to go before realizing my full potential. I even felt bad for a while for wasting so much time before I got my life in order. I now believe that no time was wasted. I was simply finding myself, my strength, and my identity. I wasn't wasting time; it was necessary time that had to be spent. The lessons that I learned from that period could be applied to all areas of life.

As a successful real estate broker, I've closed multiple sales simply by reminding myself that I've done far greater things when I was barely an adult. When I get in front of an audience to talk about my life, I sometimes feel nervous and frightened. Then I open the speech with one of the many stories from my early 20s, and I immediately feel like the crowd is a part of my story—like they all bore witness to my entire life.

I would like to encourage everyone who is experiencing difficulties in life to face them head on. We all have the strength to overcome even the greatest of hardships, and it might be that the strength is being suffocated by fear and insecurity. One thing that I discovered early on in my adult years is that strength and the power of will are like muscles. You have to train them, shape them, keep using them, and they will grow big and strong. It's easy to give up. In fact, that's the easiest thing of all the things you can do in life. Many of the things you will endure will be so stressful that it will feel as if your spine is being bent backwards. Keep reassuring yourself that as long as you try your hardest, each failure is a lesson, not a conclusion to your story.

This world is full of people; there are more than 7 billion of us. The things you are afraid of, hundreds or even thousands of people face the same fears every day. You don't need to be as successful as the best of them. You don't even need to be better than the worst of them. As long as you try your hardest, and as long as you gather the strength to go at it again after you fail, you are on the right track. You can either give up on life, or you can choose to adapt and survive.

I have been on the verge of giving up many times, but I persevered because God, fate, or whatever you want to call it, gave me the strength to realize that this is not the end—something good was going to come out of it. I had a dream, just like the one that Martin Luther King once had, a real dream that changed the course of my life forever just like his changed America forever. This was the most monumental event I had ever experienced; and this time I was aware of it. I recognized it and it changed me forever!

Chapter 2 – Exercise

1. Do you believe you are strong? Honestly tell the truth.

   Yes

2. Have you had something that was awful happen to you and were able to take away a lesson from it?

   I got Sarcoma Cancer 10 years ago. I think having Cancer makes you think about Surviving. You can give up or you can fight Cancer and come out the other side.

3. Has the lesson made you stronger or bitter and weaker? There is a difference.

   I think stronger.

"While out to sea, a large boat became shipwrecked and there was only a single survivor. This man prayed and asked God to save his life. Soon thereafter, another boat came by and offered the man some help.

"No thanks," he said. "I'm waiting for God to save me."

The men on the boat shrugged their shoulders and continued.

As the man became more deeply concerned, another boat came by. Again, the people aboard offered this man some help, and again he politely declined. "I'm waiting for God to save me," he said again.

After some time, the man began to lose faith, and soon after he died. Upon reaching Heaven, he had a chance to speak with God briefly.

"Why did you let me die? Why didn't you answer my prayers?"

"Dummy, I sent you two boats to save you!"

— Spiritual anecdote - unknown author

"Follow your instincts. Thats where true wisdom manifests itself."

— Oprah Winfrey

III. LETTING GO OF FEAR

I often wonder about soldiers who suffer from PTSD after surviving horrific events. You would think that I, of all people, would understand having trouble focusing on life or being able to sleep at night. The sleeping part was particularly puzzling to me because I usually sleep like a baby. I don't dream about the struggles I survived, and I don't have nightmares about my past; nothing like that. So you can imagine how struck Charles was when I woke up in the middle of the night, soaking wet and visibly disturbed. He knew it had to be something serious. As he poured me a glass of water, he calmly asked me what was wrong. I barely uttered that I had a dream that something bad was going to happen. He asked me if I knew what that *something* was. I told him I didn't know.

That was the first time I hid something from him. The truth is that the majority of people tell the white lies on the odd occasion, but I never kept anything from Charles, not ever.

This was a big thing.

You see, that night, I dreamt that Charles died. That's the first time I ever had a dream like that. I had trouble sleeping over the next couple of days and even though Charles was out most nights due to the nature of his work, he sensed that I was on edge about something, and couldn't hide the fact that he was worried. About a week later, he asked me again about the dream. He asked me if I had any idea about the bad thing that was going to happen, and I told him that I didn't know. That prompted one of the most sincere conversations in my entire life. We sat down at the table and he lit a cigarette, something he never did in the kitchen. He told me that he had a great life—one that he chose—and if tomorrow everything would end, he would die a happy man. The way he saw it, his life story wasn't a sad one. He also told me that he wanted to be cremated when he died.

Charles once again, just like at that pool hall, leveled me with a single look and a couple of words. Exactly a week later, as he prepared for a nap before going to the pool hall, he looked me in the eyes and asked me, "Was it about me?" And I replied, "I don't know. But you know I love you."

My six-year-old son and I were lying on the floor watching television while Charles was sleeping on the couch. At some point, our son dozed off and, not wanting to wake him up, I kept him cradled in my lap. I felt calm for the first time in weeks, and soon after dozed off as well.

Then it happened.

We were awakened by Charles falling on the top of us. He wasn't breathing, and I couldn't even feel his pulse. I immediately called an ambulance and started performing CPR, but all I could think of was the dream I had. How could that be? How could I have dreamt about it and then it really happened? As I kept trying to keep the blood coursing through his veins, I could feel him underneath my fingers; he was warm, he was there, but he wasn't. It was like he was an empty shell. His soul was already gone. As the paramedics laid him on a stretcher and wheeled him into the ambulance, I remember questioning in my head, *should I have told him about the dream?* The mind can go to unwanted places when you experience highly stressful situations. They told me to follow them to the hospital. As I drove behind them, I remembered the conversation we had in the kitchen. It was as if he was saying goodbye right there and then. Years after, I even had a suspicion that he had dreamt it as well. If he did, he hid it really well.

They said he was pronounced dead on arrival. I just sat there, shocked and dismayed, and all I could think about was the dream and the feeling I had for two weeks. I've been sensitive to this stuff before, but never have I experienced anything as severe as this. Who dreams of a person dying and then sees it happen two weeks later?

The immediate days after his death were the hardest for my kids. They were numb and devastated. Charles was a good dad, and he really loved them with all of his heart. He showed them affection in his own way. They knew they were loved, despite all the hardships we endured. I too was devastated. I never felt as lonely as I felt during those days. This was another blow that I had to take on the chin, but I knew that I had to keep moving forward. The more I thought about everything that had happened, the more I was convinced that the dream I had was a direct sign from God. I grew convinced that there was a plan for me and that I was given a sign to prepare myself.

It worked.

I was able to say my piece, and Charles got to say his, too. Who knows if we would have had that conversation if it wasn't for that dream? During this period, I learned to look differently at faith, and I changed my perspective on a lot of things. It gave me the peace of mind that because God showed me the sign by sending me that dream, I got the chance to prepare myself for what was about to happen. My last words to Charles were "I love you", and it was the best way to say goodbye to him.

It took me about a month to process it all, and that it was one of the most important periods in my life. I knew that something had to change, and that I would have to change. During all those years I spent with Charles, I had big ideas, I had plans, and I regained hope and a desire to create something worthwhile. It's as if I never listened to the voice whispering deep inside me. It was during that month of fog and haze after Charles passed that I figured that out. I knew that if I failed to follow my heart after what had just happened to me, I might have died as well with Charles.

All I had to do is let go of the fear.

For years I failed to identify fear as the main reason for not following my instinct, for not following what God was telling me all along. This was my boat. This was the time to start the next chapter of my life. This is where I decided that I would do whatever it took to achieve what I set my mind to. Many people sail through life never getting to this point. You can see now why I consider this as one of the most important periods of my life.

Charles died on Oct 5th, and by December I had enrolled in school to become a personal trainer. There were also classes on how to become a real estate agent and I felt a strong calling for that as well. Things were really tough; I struggled so much with managing two young kids at home and finishing the courses, but I wasn't going to give up no matter what. I passed the licensing test for a personal trainer, but failed the real estate one. It was hard and I was making a lot of mistakes. Every blow I took like a champ, and I moved on, learning, and adapting. I started training clients and was working as a waitress at the same time because I wasn't making enough to support my kids. They seemed to be doing fine and I did the best I could. I also sent them to counseling sessions to help them process and overcome their father's death. I was alone, and occasionally I got some help from a kind woman who was the mom of one of my daughter's friends. However, for the majority of that time, it was me and children, against the world. The thing that kept my spirits up was the fact that the progress was visible, albeit in the smallest of increments; we could see a way out. I was reading a lot of Wayne Dyer and Zig Ziglar books. I felt connected to them and a lot of the fear I felt those early days was dissipated by the quotes from their books. In a way, their books gave me hope in the same way that Charles could.

I thought about my life most nights and I recognized a lot of missed signs from God. The more I thought about it, the more I became grateful for the dream I had. It made me realize that I needed to be more aware of the messages He sends me. I needed to start following my heart and work on important stuff, on myself, on my kids, and let go of any fears and doubts. You cannot see the beauty of the rain if you are afraid of the thunder. I started living my life according to my beliefs, and it paid dividends as I learned more about myself with each passing day. I never got the chance to dream of a career when I was a kid, so there was a good chance that being a personal trainer is something I may never have become. I found my first professional passion in it. One of my clients confessed to me that my work helped her get her life back on track. Not only did she get back in shape, but she made decisive moves regarding her career and love life as well. This was perhaps the first time in my life that I felt proud of myself in such a way. I made a positive change in someone else's life.

I helped them make the change on their own.

I soon realized that my true calling in life was to help people. I don't know if that had something to do with my incredibly difficult past, but I started to believe that to be the case. Suddenly, all my hardships and the torture I survived as a teenager, all the struggles I endured with Charles, they all fell into perspective. That was God's plan all along. I needed to go through all of that to realize that my true passion was helping people overcome their troubles.

Over the years, I've come to the realization that the ability to help people is something we all possess. We all have it. We all can help others, but first we have to help ourselves. The baggage we all carry weighs heavily on us if we try to fly.

It's been decades since Charles passed, and I am still drawing lessons from it. My message to all of you is that you need to let go of your fears and listen, really listen to your intuition, your conscience, your heart, your God. I used to say, "Only God knows how I was able to survive all of that at the age of 24." I don't say that anymore, because *I* know. I know how I did it. I know what was necessary and how I made it happen. All I did was listen to God. I didn't miss the boats that came to my rescue. I missed so many before due to fear or insecurity, shame, laziness, whatever the excuse of the day was. Then I stopped making excuses and started pushing forward. My incredible kids helped me a lot just by not being *normal*. What I mean by that is that they were extraordinary. Everything I faced, they faced it with me. Every punch I received, they nursed the wounds and lifted me back up.

It was God's plan all along, and it took just one dream for me to start listening.

Chapter 3 – Exercise

1. Can you think of a time in your life that seemed to be an "ending"?

   I feel like Mike's journey with Alzheimers seems like an ending. Things slowly get worse. I have a hard time feeling hopeful.

2. What were your thoughts feelings and emotions at the time?

   Great Grief. Like I am grieving my marriage and my life.

3. Did this "ending" lead to a new beginning? What happened?

   Not sure yet

4. Think of the current challenges you face - are any of them disguised as an opportunity?

I don't know. I try to feel hopeful about Olivia. I watch my granddaughter alot. She goes to daycare on Fridays. She is a positive thing in my life.

Burn the boats and take the island

-Tony Robbins

IV. TAKING THE FIRST STEPS

I left Vegas thinking I would never go back. It wasn't the bad memories that made me think this way, I had quite many good ones, I even had a couple of great ones. <u>New opportunities in life sometimes require leaving everything behind and starting again.</u> That was the idea behind leaving. However, once again, fate bestowed upon me a change that I didn't see coming. By then, I was already convinced that every decision I made was the right one. Not literally, because everyone makes mistakes, but I was 100% sure that even when I did make a bad decision, if the reasoning was in line with my logic and backed by my intuition, or as I like to call it, <u>*a blessing from God*</u>, it was meant to be. All the mistakes, all the mishaps, all the suffering, the Golgotha I survived, every single moment in my life played a part in shaping me into the person I was back then.

By 2004, I liked myself.

I honestly liked the face, the expression, the person, the survivor who gazed back at me in the mirror. I made enough money to keep my kids safe and sound, and not in need of anything. My clients were happy, and I enjoyed my work to the point that if you would have asked me if I was happy with my life, the answer would have most certainly been "yes". I had come a long way from being chained and locked in a closet contemplating if I should keep fighting or give up. If I could single out the greatest gift I received from God, it would definitely be the fact that even back then, I knew that there was more for me out there.

I had a purpose.

It takes some people decades to realize that, and many never even get to that point. I just imagined and wished for normalcy for most of my hardship-stricken life. A peaceful life where I was surrounded by people who didn't have bad intentions for me—a direct result of desiring something I didn't have as a kid. Now that I had it, and even more since I was surrounded by people who genuinely cared about me as much as I cared about them, I knew there was more. Once again, it was a single stroke of God's brilliance and one simple message that showed me that I was capable and destined for greater things. This may sound like a narcissistic and delusional person's statement of grandeur. If it does, remember what I said about my life and everything I went through. I'm extremely proud today, and back then, of everything I've accomplished in my life. I don't need or require other people's approval to value my success and consider it as extraordinary as I do.

You don't have to, either.

Success is a relative and a subjective term. Remind yourself of that every day, and you will soon realize how powerful you can be.

Let's get back to the sign that created another tidal wave in my life, prompting me to once again start from scratch. I was living in Miami at the time. My social life wasn't as eventful for a period of time; that was until I met David. He was a police officer and a really sweet guy. We dated for a while, and we enjoyed each other's company. He met my kids, and we were spending a lot of time together. However, I wasn't 100% sure about him. There was something about him that I simply couldn't get completely comfortable with. I think part of my feeling was that he was a police officer and was always very suspicious of his surroundings. It wasn't like he was always looking out for signs of something bad, but it was his way of thinking and how he viewed the world.

Let's look at it another way: If I, with all the history of betrayal and abuse, have more faith and trust in people than you, then you may need to re-examine your view of the world. He would question everything, and I never felt like he completely trusted me. Love and partnership are more about the trust than mutual affection, and so this wasn't sitting right with me. Yes, he was passionate, he cared about me, and I had strong feelings for him, but that little shadow of a doubt was stopping me from taking things with him to the next level; his doubt about me made me doubt my future with him.

By this time in my life, I knew better. I wanted more and I was taking the first steps, including steps toward a relationship, to make my life's goals and path focused toward achieving happiness. Once again, I was given a clear sign, a clear message and I remember it like it happened yesterday. On New Year's Eve, I was with my oldest daughter and her friend, who were both 18 at the time, baking cupcakes. We had some laughs, genuinely had a good time, and seeing as it was New Year's, I was questioning my life and my choices and was thinking about those silly resolutions people usually make. As I was thinking about my life, I went to the bedroom and prayed for a while, something I did whenever I faced uncertainty of any kind.

This time, it was about David. I asked God to help me with this decision. I asked him to help find my soulmate, and I said it out loud. I knew it as soon as I uttered the words that it wasn't David. That would have been good enough for me if it had stopped there, but God once again smiled down upon me and guided me in the right direction. You often hear the saying *God works in mysterious ways*.

Well, I can guarantee you that this is every bit as true as it reads. His message for me crystal clear and undeniable.

Go back to Vegas, and there you'll find your soul mate.

I left Vegas thinking I would never return, but right then and there, the decision was made. I was going back. I knew better than not to listen to that voice and not to take God's advice. This was perhaps one of the last critical points in my life, the last milestone where I had to muster up enough courage and start all over again. There was no doubt in my heart about it. The move back to Vegas had to happen.

As I walked out of the bedroom, I sat down with my daughter and told her about my decision because I needed confirmation to make it final. As I revealed my intentions to her, she didn't think about it for more than a few seconds. She looked me in the eyes and told me, "Your intuition had been always right, the messages you were given have never failed you, I think you should follow it again." And that was it. That's all I needed. Over the next couple of weeks, I packed my things, and within two months I moved back to Las Vegas. I wasn't thrilled about it, it wasn't easy for me, but I knew it was the right choice. I knew what that move would do for my life. I had to start all over again, rebuild everything I had left in Miami. I knew that I would have to make new clients, and that I would probably struggle financially for some time. I knew that my entire life was now on a hard reset, but I didn't care. It was the right choice.

It was the right choice.

I was lucky enough to land a job as soon as I got to Las Vegas. I started training new clients, and I even got a morning job assisting at a finance company that dealt with loans. Each night I prayed asking for discernment and direction. That went on for weeks, and each time I prayed I was looking the smallest of clues on what to do next.

IV. TAKING THE FIRST STEPS

Then God spoke.

I switched from the gym where I was working for one that I'd never been to before. Not much changed after the switch, but I wasn't giving up. I traveled across town every day for work, sometimes even twice a day, but I wasn't fazed by it, because all the while, the voice was telling me *it's the right choice*.

Determination is one of my most dominant character traits, especially when I think back on all the things I've survived without giving up. I survived with my mom being drunk all the time, survived a sexually abusive foster dad, survived being sentenced to a juvenile detention center; I wasn't broken by vicious pimps and evil men, and I kept my head held high when Charles died leaving me with two small kids and no money. A change in cities? A change of jobs? This was a cake walk compared to those things. I could do this for decades and not give up. It had nothing to do with the degree of difficulty; it was the fact that this, out of all previous things, was the thing *I* chose. It's one thing to survive and accept the hardships when you don't have control over them. It's a completely different thing when you choose to follow your gut, your instinct, pursuing true happiness in life. It's easy to give up when you don't need to face the struggles, but choose to.

I would like to encourage you to start doing it more often. That's why this chapter is called *Taking the First Steps*. I am not advising you to leave your job and move to Vegas taking a shot as a professional gambler. Or moving to Hawaii to become a writer and a surfing instructor. Don't make rash decisions that could backfire because you were not sure about it in the first place. In fact, most of your decisions should never be judged based on the outcome.

Start listening to your heart, your intuition, your God.

Start making decisions that you will feel good about regardless of the outcome. Look deep inside your soul and figure out what it is that really makes you happy, and work toward that. I did a drastic thing because I was already used to starting over, but you don't have to be like me in order to take those first steps. Think about your true desires, devise a plan, talk to your family about it, and if you can't make it happen that moment, take at least the first step. Work toward it, and even if you fail, it won't be for the lack of trying or not trying at all.

Just take that first step.

I did, and it wasn't easy, but that was the right thing to do. While I was swinging and missing, I kept looking for clues and for new messages that would guide me down that path. That's why I was surprised that it was not the next message that changed my life forever; it was the piercing, clanging sound like when metal smashes against metal that changed my life forever.

Chapter 4 – Exercise

If you knew that you could not fail, what would your future look like? I want you to dream big and fill in your visions below.

_____
_____
_____
_____
_____
_____
_____
_____
_____
_____
_____
_____
_____
_____
_____
_____
_____
_____

Whether you think you can or you can't, you're right.

— Henry Ford

V. GOING AFTER WHAT YOU WANT

Do you ever watch nature programs that show all sorts of animals gathering at a single watering place? I always found it interesting that nature attracts so many different species to the same place like in the African savanna. It's where an abundance of life meets the scarcity of the resources. The herd of antelopes knows that there are predators like lions, pumas, crocodiles, and hyenas just waiting for them, but they risk it anyway. There is plenty to be taken from a situation like this. That scene represents life. You are in the herd and you can stay in the pack, in the middle, hoping that the pack moves just enough toward the water for you to have a sip. Even if that happens, it's the water most of the pack had already stepped in, meaning it's dirty and polluted. That is the approach most people take in life. They stay within the bubble, hoping to scrape by and counting on getting lucky in order to get a sip of that fresh cold water, which it rarely is.

By the time I moved back to Las Vegas, I was no longer a part of the herd. In fact, I was way ahead of it. I knew that if I survived, I'd find the spot where there were no crocodiles, no lions, with pure, fresh water that I could sip from all day long for the rest of my life. The other thing I've always found fascinating about the savanna environment is that all the animals have an acute sense of good versus bad. Even though the herd is surrounded by an incredible level of noise with thousands of hooves stomping on the ground, every gazelle, with all that noise around, hears the subtle sound of a lion running at them at full speed from hundreds of yards away. It is in their blood, it is in their destiny. The reason why I draw this comparison is that I firmly believe that we are all like gazelles. We all hear that subtle sound, that subtle voice, that is whispering, *hey, here comes the danger* or *hey, this is the best thing for you.*

We just choose not to listen to it.

Our choice prevents us from either moving out of harm's way, or from stepping into the boat that God sent to save us from drowning.

I was recently speaking with a client of mine, and we were rambling on about the difference between morning and evening workouts. There were literally dozens of people around us, and it seemed like it was one of the busiest days I've ever seen at the gym. The noise was literally overwhelming. As we were talking, I heard a loud sound that came from somewhere behind me. It was as deafening as thunder. I ducked down instantly and turned around. Someone had dropped a kettle bell, and as I turned and scanned the room, more instinctively than consciously, I saw him. He was standing next to a water fountain. You know how angels and saints are usually depicted with a halo around their head? This man had a halo around him. As I was staring at him, my client interrupted my gaze and asked if I was okay. As I turned toward her, I noticed that she wasn't fazed by the loud sound. In fact, no one in the building seemed to be bothered by it. I asked her, "Did you hear that?" She looked at me with an expression of someone who had been asked if they knew how to convert light years into miles. "Hear what? Is everything ok? You seem erratic." I didn't even respond. I turned back around and watched as this man took a sip of water from the fountain. It felt like everything else stopped. I don't even know how the conversation my client and I were having even ended. I drove home, went straight to my bedroom, got on my knees, and said my prayers, ending with, "I heard you. Thank you."

During the hour-long drive home that day, I figured out that what happened in the gym was a sign from God. No one else heard the sound that I did. No one turned around. No one flinched. It was meant just for me. I knew right away that the man was my soulmate. I was sure of it. I had a hard time falling asleep that night as I was anxious to return to the gym. I didn't see him the next morning, but I did during my afternoon workout. I saw him at the water fountain again. I tried to get his attention, but he didn't notice me. I came back the next day armed with my cutest workout outfit—one that I bought to get his attention—no success. I must have walked past him a dozen times, but he didn't even give me a glimpse. About two weeks of later, still with no success, I decided to change up my game plan.

Desperate times call for desperate measures.

So, when he walked to the water fountain that day, I followed him and stood so close to him that he got startled. I was like a penguin.

What does a penguin have to do with this?

Male penguins do this when courting—they search the beach for the cutest pebble they can find to present it to their chosen mate. Instead of a pebble, I had a paper cup. I hate water fountains, by the way, and I noticed he always drank from it without a cup. When I startled him, he turned around and asked me, "Do you want to go first?" Then he really saw me. I could see in his eyes the moment that he noticed me. You know the feeling when you notice someone for the first time. No matter how long you know their face or their eyes. There is a distinct moment when you notice them in a different light. I caught that in his eyes. It took him a second to gather and introduce himself as Viktor. I asked him if he wanted to use my cup. He took it. I knew it right there that he was my soulmate. I believe he did as well.

I waited for him outside the gym that evening. I wasn't going to let this man walk out of there without knowing that we would meet again. If there was ever a time that Viktor thought I was a psychopath, it was the moment he saw me standing outside next to his motorcycle. Again, he was startled, judging by his mannerisms, but he got over it fairly quickly. It was obvious that I was interested in him since I was waiting for him, but I wasn't yet sure if he was interested in me. After talking for a while, he asked, "Can I take you out sometime?" I was already 2-weeks deep into him. In fact, I was already years into him since I knew he was my soulmate. I fell in love with him as soon as I started imaging our life together. So I replied, "How about now?" There was an obstacle. He was working as a bouncer that night until midnight. I didn't let go. "That works for me, call me." And we went our separate ways.

Remember, I never went to high school, so this was my girly-teen freak out stage. I was sitting overexcited in my home, thinking, *"Will he call me? Will he call me? He will, will he? He has to, he asked me out, he's going to call!"* There I was, a grown woman with a couple of kids and an entire lifetime behind me, freaking out about a boy like a teenage girl. I still smile from ear to ear every time I recall that moment.

11.55 PM. Those 5 minutes took longer than the weeks I spent chained in the dark with the savage who tortured me when I was 16.

12.01 AM. My phone rings.

We met at a bar and grill and had ice teas. It was one of those conversations that could have lasted forever. He told me about his life, and I told him about mine. He told me that he was in the Air

Force, and he mentioned that he had to be back at the base by 6:00 am. Plenty of time, right? Well, we talked for 5 hours straight without missing a beat. That was it, we knew it, we both did. He rushed back home to get his uniform and went to work. He called me that day every chance he got. I often think about that day, and it really is the cornerstone of my life. At that moment, everything made perfect sense. I realized that my entire life simply had to happen exactly the way it did for me to meet Viktor.

I was at peace with it. I still am.

There is a thing called 'The Law of Vibration'. We will get into this in more detail later, but this law basically explains that everything around us vibrates. You attract, and are attracted to, people that vibrate the same way as you. Viktor and I recognized the fact that we were in sync immediately. In fact, 6 weeks after we met, we were married. 14 years later, we still look at each other like we did at that water fountain.

I never was a skeptic, and I've always strived to have a positive perspective on life. By all accounts, I could have been a misanthrope considering all that I have suffered through and survived. However, many people do walk down that subtle path of misanthrope. If any of you that follow me on this journey are in a spot where you are about to give up—don't! The reason this chapter is called *Going After What You Want* is quite literal—that's the way out. I was the gazelle in front of the herd, looking for that fresh water patch. You can be, too. I am not advising you to take big risks, to throw away everything you have accomplished and hold dear seeking for your true passion. That is acceptable only if you are 100% certain of what your passion is and that it will make you happy. Even then, you have to plan it out and be prepared to thick-skin it for a while. Start stepping outside of your comfort zone and begin taking decisive steps toward the things you are passionate about. If you would like to meet a person that will complete your life, you have to open yourself up a bit. Don't wait for that person, search for them. When you find that person, don't stand around waiting for them to make the first move. Do it yourself.

Wait outside by their motorcycle if you have to!

If you are not willing to fight for what you desire, do you really deserve it? My life, my actions, my story, can be yours, too. Not to wish upon anyone some of the events that I survived, but each and every one of you can recall a situation in your life where you felt as I did. Who's to say that your grief, that your anger, that your despair was greater or smaller than mine? The cause of an event and your feelings only matter if you recognize them and take action based on that recognition.

Let me explain it this way. Cardiovascular diseases kill way more people than cancer does. However, cancer is the most feared disease ever. The reason is because there are no definite answers about what causes cancer. When you survive a heart attack, you know that it is either stress, unhealthy diet, lack of exercise, or a genetic cause. That's it. If you stay away from the first three, it is highly unlikely that the fourth one will have an effect on you. With cancer, after you survive it, unless you are a smoker, you are left clueless as to what caused it and what actions you should take to make sure that it doesn't come back.

Causes matter to us.

In fact, as babies, we learn using two methods: mimicking the environment and figuring out the cause and effect results. So when I say *step outside your comfort zone*, what I really mean is *don't be complacent about the causes influencing your life*. Go after you want, whatever size steps you can manage, just start walking toward it. You will make mistakes and plenty of them. I was making mistakes for the first two weeks with Viktor. No results; hit and miss.

I didn't quit. I kept swinging.

> *Many of life's failures are people who did not realize how close they were to success when they gave up.*
>
> —Thomas A. Edison

Viktor and I have been married for 14 years, and we have 5 beautiful children together. I have followed him around the globe. He was stationed in Germany for four years, did two tours in Iraq. Each of those events required me to step ahead of the herd once again and keep searching, keep fighting, keep going after the things that I wanted, that I needed, that made me happy. Success feels so much better when you know it is well-earned. There was a study published in 2012 that stated that the rate of self-made millionaires that go bankrupt versus the ones who inherit (win a lottery or a lawsuit, who do not earn it) the money and go bust is 1:17. That means that if you get something without working for it, without achieving it on your own, you are 17 times more likely to lose it for the lack of appreciation or the smarts to keep it. So go out there and work for it, go after what you want, and if you do fail, it won't feel as bitter as spending the rest of your life wondering about what could have happened if you tried.

Don't get complacent.

I consider myself a successful person, a mother, a wife, a businesswoman, but I keep listening to that voice over and over again, *"Is there something else I want in life? What is it, where can I find it? What do I need to do to make it happen?"* I keep finding it.

It feels better than money, better than status, better than any drug in the world. I keep finding things that I want, and once I work for them and get them, it's the best feeling in the world. At this moment, it's sharing my experience with people who struggle that drives me forward. If I am to continue being happy in life, I need to know that I am still ready to do whatever it takes for the things that the voice inside me whispers. In fact, when Viktor retired, things got a bit tight again. I made the decision to succeed, and despite the housing market collapse, despite the economic turmoil that swept the entire world, I kept hammering, and I finally made it. I had to go through everything that I did in order to do that. I expect loads of bumps on the roads ahead, but you know what? Let them come.

Chapter 5 – Exercise

What are 5 things that you want to manifest into your life?

1.

2.

3.

4.

5.

Out of those 5, what is your big WHY? Why do you want it and why is it so important?

1.

2.

3.

4.

5.

My goal is not to be better than anyone else, but to be better than I used to be.

-—— Wayne Dyer

VI. FORGIVING YOURSELF

Success can be a strange phenomenon. What I've come to understand is that unless you earn and deserve it, but more importantly, unless you share it, it tends to lose some of its meaning. This is especially true when you take into account that being successful in the business world is only the half of the story. It is usually that the other half of the story is more important. If your life is not complete physically, spiritually, and emotionally, money can be quite meaningless. In fact, in many cases, financial wealth can quickly lead a person to unimaginable depths if their life is not balanced. It is easier to walk through life with loving friends and family that support you, in good health and spirit, than with millions in the bank but surrounded by people who don't hear your inner voice. I would rather be a beggar on the street than to suffer in silence in a 12-bedroom mansion. Over the years of coaching clients, I concluded that we all need to stay balanced and forgive ourselves for all the mistakes we've made. You cannot forgive others without first forgiving yourself.

Viktor and I got married in 2005. We weren't planning to get married that day; we just wanted to get the wedding license. Once we arrived, we figured, *why put it off?* We called our closest family and friends and gave them a two-hour notice. In some ways it was the wedding of my dreams.

I'm not that kind of a girly girl who imagined a huge wedding, a lavish white gown, white doves and all that. Considering that at the age when girls usually fantasize about those things, I was being held captive, beaten, and forced into prostitution; it's surprising that I actually got married at all. This was truly the wedding of my dreams because it was all about me and Viktor. Nothing else mattered. No one else mattered.

It was very strange being married to a military man. Soon after we got married, Viktor had his first deployment to Iraq. He was gone for 9 months, and at first it was really hard on me. There I was, finally settled with a man who provides me peace and comfort, who excites me with a simple smile, who understands the way I think and operate. Yet, I was living alone in Vegas. I knew better than to think negative about it because after all the hardships I had endured, I knew this was only a part of the plan that God had in store for me. In a way, it was as if I received a period of solitude to figure out what my next moves should be. I used the time wisely and read tons of books, attended seminars, constantly improving the way I saw myself. I knew it at the time that there still were things that I needed to work on. In a way, those nine months were a boot camp for the other parts of my life. I needed to find that balance and figure out how to maintain it.

I thought about my mother quite often, especially during the days when I first became a mother myself. I held a grudge for a long time and it was weighing me down. I needed to mend that relationship if I was ever going to be truly happy about my life. To be completely honest, it wasn't as hard as one would imagine. It was far from easy, but the thing I took for granted for the better part of my life was that everyone has their own story. I vaguely knew my mom's story, but it wasn't until I learned about the details from my aunt that I fully comprehended what her life was really like.

My mother was born in Latvia and was 8 years old when World War

VI. FORGIVING YOURSELF

II was raging throughout Europe. She was in and out refugee camps in constant fear for almost 5 years. So in a way, she survived a similar tragedy as me; only she was younger than I was at the time. She witnessed several of her friends and family members being taken to concentration camps and eventually killed, and her life was a misery. It got so bad that she couldn't sleep at all from the anxiety and the fear of being taken as well. So, her mom gave her a teaspoon of alcohol every night to help her settle down and catch at least an hour of sleep. You cannot blame my grandmother for that; she did the best she could. In a way, my mom was destined to be an alcoholic. It was the only coping mechanism she ever knew. I often contemplated what her life must have been like. For me to be born in America, my mother had to be guided by God as well. My entire family ended up in America under a very fortunate set of events. They received help packages from the Red Cross, and it was the only way to survive the aftermath of the war. The system was random, so you would never know if you would be given a package or not. One day, my mother grabbed one of the packages and refused to let it go. She wasn't going to be given one that day, but seeing her distressed to the point of being deranged, they decided to let her have it. I don't know what forced my mom to pick that package and do what she did; I can only speculate that she heard the same inner voice as I did.

That was the package that brought her to the United States.

Inside the package was a purple ladies coat, and in the pocket of that coat was a note stating that the sender of the package would sponsor the entire family to come to America. A couple of months later, they were on a ship heading to the United States.

Once I had kids of my own, and especially when Viktor was stationed in Germany where we lived for 4 years, I gained a new perspective on a lot of things. One of them is the importance of family and the role they play in your life. I repaired all the damage with my mom, and send her nothing but love. If it wasn't for her, I would have never been what I am today. You see, I decided that the cycle of misfortune both of us endured as kids would end with me. If I hadn't done that, then all of her suffering and mine as well would have been in vain as none of us would have ever found peace. It was liberating to forgive her, and to forgive myself. I should have done it a lot sooner. I spent a lot of time with her sister as well. I never really had a chance to bond with my other cousins. I never knew my father and I only met him once. He died two weeks after I met him so once again, I felt like it was God's plan for me to meet him and say goodbye. All of these small nuances that I constantly experience re-affirm my faith and keep proving to me that I am on the right path.

My mom died shortly after my dad passed away, and I still mention her in every one of my prayers. With all that she was, she was my mom; she was the one that I have so much to be thankful for, both good and bad. She is partly the reason I have the life I can be proud of.

One of the things that fulfills me the most is helping people. If you only consider my career as a personal trainer and a life coach, you can see that it's not just a job for me. It's my calling in life—I am destined to do this. For the longest time I was struggling to find inner peace until I figured out that I still held a grudge against myself for various reasons, big and small. Gradually, I learned to let them go one by one, and it felt liberating. You will never reach your full potential until you get rid of all the anger, disappointments, any ill feelings toward others and yourself. Learn to forgive yourself for making mistakes, and you will learn to forgive others. Once you have finally done it, your entire perspective will shift, and it will free you to pursue things that are really important to you. The reason I can give advice about any of this is that I learned it myself, the hard way. I never had any formal education worth mentioning, but the harshness of life schooled me better than any college ever could. These ideas and constructs I talk about are not some philosophies that I

VI. FORGIVING YOURSELF

decided I would base this book on. They are my life, summed up in lessons which shaped me into the person I am today. When I experienced love for the first time with Charles, he wasn't the love of my life, but it felt good. I was struggling financially. When I dated David, the business was good, but he wasn't the man I could honestly love. When Viktor retired, I had everything in place. I was emotionally satisfied; I was loved by him, by my kids, by my family and friends. The business wasn't as good, but I knew that it would eventually pick up because I was balanced. Everything has been just where it needed to be. Step by step, I climbed to the top 1% of all the real estate brokers in the United States. My coaching was going well. I considered myself successful.

The missing piece was the forgiveness.

"One day Buddha walked through a village. A very angry and rude young man came up and began insulting him.

"You have no right teaching others, he shouted. *You are as stupid as everyone else. You are nothing but a fake."*

Buddha was not upset by these insults. Instead, he asked the young man: *"Tell me, if you buy a gift for someone and that person does not take it, to whom does the gift belong?"*

The man was surprised to be asked such a strange question and answered: *"It would belong to me because I bought the gift."*

The Buddha smiled and said: *"That is correct. And it is exactly the same with your anger. If you become angry with me and I do not get insulted, then the anger falls back on you. You are the only one who becomes unhappy, not me. All you have done is hurt yourself."*

The man looked all confused.

The Buddha continued: *"If you want to stop hurting yourself, you must get rid of your anger and become loving instead. When you hate others, you yourself become unhappy. But when you love others*, the Buddha smiled, *everyone is happy."*

— Unknown author

VI. FORGIVING YOURSELF

Life is never going to be easy, and I cannot attest to yours. No one but you can know what your life feels like. All I can do is share my story and the lessons I've learned. Many of you might not recognize your life situation in my story and link it to my experience, but the feelings are certainly relatable, because these feelings are universal. These feelings level us all and when someone is struggling internally, all the worldly possessions, all the wealth, it means nothing. The reason why I said earlier that financial wealth can sometimes lead to unimaginable depths is because an unhappy person will often seek the solution in the bottom of a bottle or in drugs. That cycle lasts far longer when you have the money to invest in it.

It is important to understand the role you have played in your failures in life before you put any of the blame and burden on others. Whether I talk to a client in a private session, or stand on the podium in front of hundreds of people, I can admit without any shame or regret that I need help as well. Self-help. Half of the solution, a number of rehab programs will tell you, is in the recognition that the problem exists in the first place. I've read dozens of self-help books and I have attended many seminars, and I still think about my life and the choices I have made. I still occasionally need help. In the moments I feel like life is weighing me down, I ask for guidance—from Viktor, my sons and daughters, my friends, and from God as well. That is the thing I want all of you to ponder. In each and every one of us, there is tremendous strength. We are capable of extraordinary things, each in our own way.

You need balance in life in order to shine.

I once had a client who was a tremendous singer, one of the best I've ever heard. Her future came into question because she wasn't eating right. She would wake up, drink 5-6 cups of coffee, and maybe eat an apple. For weeks she did this, and it started to affect her voice. She had no strength to carry it out, even though she was one of the strongest women I've met in my entire life. As we started working out, she would outwork me every session. With no strength in her body, she lifted twice as much as I did. I knew there was something deeper that bothered her. A few weeks into the coaching, she started crying in the middle of the session; she cried for an hour. After she calmed down a bit, she told me that was the first time she had cried in 11 years. She opened up and said that she lost a brother in a car accident when she was 13. He was taking her to the supermarket after she begged him for hours and he finally agreed. She blamed herself for years, and it took her almost 6 months of sessions to completely get it out of her system. She now has 5 successful albums and is in better shape than some Olympic sprinters. She is eating healthy, she visits her brother's grave every month (after not visiting for 11 years), and she is happily engaged. In order for her to have taken that final step in her career, she needed that balance, as we all do. I could have told you my story in a much longer format than these 6 chapters, but it's not a story worth simply re-telling. I really feel like I struck the balance in life and I want you all to try and do the same. The next 6 chapters will be focused on some of the constructs that I, knowingly or not, used to get to this point of my life. I really do believe that all of us are capable of being people that are greater than the life we are currently living. It's just a matter of striking that balance and listening to the inner voice that never lies.

My life story, my experience, my accomplishments—all of that laid the foundation that enabled me to build my entire identity. Between that, and help from my mentor, Wayne Dyer, to whom I'm incredibly indebted, I was able to find my inner peace, understand my strengths, my gifts, and identify, and my weaknesses. I owe a lot of the success to the people whose books I've read, and if my book helps just one person, it would be worth the effort I've put into it.

Chapter 6 – Exercise

1. Honestly, have you forgiven yourself?

2. Why are you holding onto the hurt? Has it become a normal part of your being? Do you feel a sense of power in the story? We become the stories we most tell to ourselves.

3. How would your life look without the story?

Creating a Roadmap for a Better Life

Our deepest fear is not that we are inadequate.
Our deepest fear is that we are powerful beyond measure.
It is our light, not our darkness, that most frightens us.
We ask ourselves; Who am I to be brilliant,
gorgeous, handsome, talented and fabulous?

Actually, who are you not to be?
You are a child of God.

You playing small does not serve the world.
There is nothing enlightened about shrinking
so that other people won't feel insecure around you.
We are all meant to shine, as children do.

We were born to make manifest the glory of God within us.
It is not just in some; it is in everyone.

And, as we let our own light shine, we consciously give
other people permission to do the same.
As we are liberated from our fear,
our presence automatically liberates others.

—— Marianne Williamson

VII. TRUSTING YOUR INSTINCTS

We are all different, but we all make the same mistakes. Have you ever wondered why that is? How is it that a middle-class person from Washington makes the same mistakes as a struggling mother of six in Wyoming? That's because it is in our nature. We primarily use two ways of learning as adults: deducing causes and relations by applying logical thinking, or trying to do the same thing practicing a trial and error approach. This is the reason why you make the same mistakes as most people; you probably used the wrong approach many times in your life. For example, have you ever met someone while staying out just a tad later then you should have, only to regret it? Well, that's an instance where you should have used your brain and logic, but you opted for a trial and error method. There is no need to feel bad about mistakes like these. Well, not too bad at least. There is a lesson to be learned in almost any situation, you just need to look past the pain, past the misery, the humiliation, the humor, or past the pride, which in most cases is more damaging than the all of the other factors combined.

To achieve any level of success, you need to be at peace with yourself. I found that the biggest contributors to that peace are staying honest to yourself and following your instincts. There is nothing more frustrating and disturbing when you do something against your instincts and then you have to deal with the consequences. There is a great quote I heard in a movie that is applicable in so many spheres of life: "Few players recall big pots they have won, strange as it seems, but every player can remember with remarkable accuracy the outstanding tough beats of his career." This quote is about card players, but it resonates with me a lot. I cannot remember one time that I listened to my instincts and made a mistake and ended up regretting my decision. I am haunted by the mistakes I made when I didn't listen to my instincts, and I am pretty sure that many of you feel the same. The worst sentence I have ever spoken to myself is, "*I knew it.*" That one takes me out of the balance almost as any other setback I've experienced, if not more. Mistakes I don't mind, they are the natural way of learning and improving, but when I make a mistake and I knew it was the wrong decision in the first place, that one sticks with me. Like the quote says, I can remember with remarkable accuracy the outstanding beats of my life because all of them came from the negative outcomes ending with the sentence, "*I knew it.*"

Neglecting my inner voice is not something that I do often, but just imagine if it was. Would I have ever met Viktor? Would I have ever amounted to anything in life? Luckily for me, I proved to myself early on that my instincts, my messages from God, or whatever you want to call that inner voice that whispers in your ear, provide the best advice I could ever hope for. I see so many people following the same pattern of mistakes just because they do not listen to that inner voice. We have so much more than the 5 senses we are taught. One of them is intuition, instinct, a strange kind of energy that can sense danger, that if you listen to really carefully, always works in your best interest. The only catch is distinguishing it from all the other voices in your ears and in your head. I like to call it the voice of the heart. Learning to recognize that voice and include it in the decision-making process can be a tricky thing to do.

VII. TRUSTING YOUR INSTINCTS

The problem is that many people actually misuse the word instinct and they do not realize how powerful it actually is. You must have heard it so many times that someone played a number at the roulette table because they followed their instinct. That's a very common mistake people make. A person that follows a message like that is not following their instincts because the first thing their instinct would tell them, what everybody's instinct would tell, is that you should not be playing roulette in the first place. Not to deny that gambling can be fun, but it's just that the voice I am referring to is always looking out for your best interest. There are so many subtle nuances that need to be taken into consideration that it can be really difficult to distinguish that voice from all the others, like ambition, greed, desire, attraction, etc. When you fine-tune your senses to recognize it, the messages might frighten you, scare you, and take you on a difficult path.

Your instincts are never wrong.

You can make mistakes based on those decisions, but in the long run, while you are building a happier life, your instincts are the best guidelines. If you actually imagine the roadmap of a happy life, how well you respond to your instincts will determine your level of success. When your foundation has been firmly established, the house you are building will be strong and capable of housing a greater life. When you lay foundations on shaky ground, no matter how high you build it, it will always be in danger of tumbling down.

It is hard, trust me, I know. When I left Miami and went back to Vegas, it was hard for me. It may seem like it was a walk in the park compared to the rest of the life experiences I had endured before that, but it was one of the hardest things I had ever done. Trusting your instincts can be so difficult that it feels as if you will never make it, but failing to follow those subtle messages will result in an imbalance that will prohibit you from ever achieving true happiness. You can become successful without following your instincts, but I am not talking about business success. I am talking about true happiness. I have searched for true happiness my entire life, but it wasn't until I started learning about Wayne Dyer and his work that I realized what that really means. During one of his speaking engagements that I attended, he talked about success and happiness. About a half an hour into it, I realized that I was just like every other person on the planet—chasing something that I could not define. Before that, I never really thought about what true happiness was. Over the years as I've studied his teachings, I figured out a roadmap that would work for the majority of people as well as it has worked for me. With that, let's go back to the start of this chapter.

We are all different, but we all make the same mistakes. Stop and think about it. This is the first thing everyone needs to realize before moving on to creating a better life. How do we stop making the same mistakes? Start listening to your instincts. Start making decisions based on what your true desires are, and you will start making fewer mistakes. The mistakes you do make will not hurt as much, and you will learn from them and become a better person. Your inner voice will not try and deceive you.

There is no mask that you can put on to fool yourself in to thinking that you are happy with your life.

You can only silence it for a while, and that never ends well. You can be happy to some extent if the people around you are happy, but you should never build your life like that. Imagine a life where you are happy because people around you are the ones who are happy, or because you have a lot of material things. The nature and reality of people and material things is that they both eventually leave, or simply stop being sufficient. They are temporary.

VII. TRUSTING YOUR INSTINCTS

True happiness comes from within you.

From inner peace, from the balance that weighs your actions against your instincts, and your true desires. When you strike that balance, you will make people around you happy, not the other way around. When they do eventually leave, what remains is that you are still happy.

I met a couple that lost everything during Hurricane Katrina. They were one of the happiest couples I've ever seen in my life. They lost their business, their house, their car, their jewelry, even some of their friends, but they were still happy. When I spoke with them, they told me that it wasn't the house, the car, or the business that gave meaning to their life. Those things only gave them a sense of accomplishment. "We built it once, we can rebuild it if we want to." They were able to build it because they listened to the inner voice and followed the path that it was guiding them toward. Just like that.

They were 56 and 58 years old at the time.

We talked for hours when I finally figured out why they were so calm about it. There was no "*I knew it*" after the hurricane. They weren't at odds with themselves regarding what happened. They took it on the chin and kept pushing forward. This is what I mean by a solid foundation. They are a perfect example of what I am absolutely sure of: when you build your life on a solid foundation, not even a storm as powerful as Katrina can tear it down.

The reason you need to learn the skill of following your instincts is because you need to figure out what is it that will make you happy before taking steps toward it. There is an exercise I want you to do. I want you to work backwards from this point in your life and ask yourself a couple of simple questions. *Are you truly happy with your life? If not, what is missing from it?* These two questions are harder to find answers to than you actually realize. Now here is the important part. Once you do realize what is missing from your life, ask yourself *did you lose it, or simply never had it in the first place?* And for both cases, *why?* This is where all of the masks you wear to fool yourself come off.

Then, start listening.

These are the questions your intuition has the answers to, not which number will win you the jackpot. Your instincts are designed to kick in when you ask truly fundamental questions. Answers to these questions will change everything for you, or they may not, in which case you are already truly happy, but you just don't realize it yet. This Wayne Dyer quote sums it up perfectly: *The state of your life is nothing more than a reflection of the state of your mind.*

Most of your problems can be solved by yourself. All you have to do is let go of the fear, let go of the pride, fine-tune that sensitivity to your inner voice, and start making decisions that are based on the messages that your inner voice sends you. That is the solid foundation that allows you to build a skyscraper a thousand stories high. The balance between the things you do, and the things your instincts tell you to do, will keep it from tipping over.

Chapter 7 – Life Defining Questions

Life Question 1

What are 8 things I want "to be"?

1.

2.

3.

4.

5.

6.

7.

8.

Life Question 2

What are the 8 things that I want "to do"?

1.

2.

3.

4.

5.

6.

7.

8.

Life Question 3

What are 8 things that I want "to have"?

1.

2.

3.

4.

5.

6.

7.

8.

You do not attract what you want, you attract what you are.

— Wayne Dyer

VIII. FINDING YOUR PURPOSE

It is impossible to compare the problems that we face and the degree to which they affect each of us individually. We cannot possibly know how another person experiences pain when a loved one is lost, or any of the stuff life throws at us. The same is true for success. What some people consider success, others see as an everyday occurrence. I met a soldier who saved his entire squadron from death. He lost an arm in the process and received a medal of honor. When he retired, he struggled so hard to restore a modicum of normalcy in his life and failing to find a purpose, a calling, the meaning, that it devastated him. For him, his heroic acts were not something he would consider extraordinary; it was his duty, and that was his purpose for being there. For the men he saved that day, he was one of the most accomplished men they had ever met. We are so different, but every one of us strives toward the same thing—meaning and purpose in life. Call it whatever you want. That *something* is what motivates us to keep grinding, or stops us from ever being successful.

It depends whether you've got what it takes to find it.

We all do a lot of things on autopilot, not thinking about the reasons for doing what we do. Most of us have a general idea of where we are headed. That is better than not having a clue at all, but it is still not enough to be truly happy. This is a real issue many people come face to face with when they least expect it. I spoke about this a great deal with Viktor, as he understands the military lifestyle and effects. I also spoke about it with the soldier who saved all those lives. He spoke about his time in the military—a place where he knew exactly what needed to be done, exactly at what time, how precise—every single detail. That was his life. He had a purpose. After retiring, he was still a young, vibrant man, but he lost that sense of purpose. He was engaged to a beautiful woman, and they were financially stable and lived comfortably. But he lost the sense of purpose in his life and it left a huge void that he so desperately tried to fill. He told me that being home at 10:00 am and not knowing what he should be doing that day was 10 times worse than being shot at by a bunch of bloodthirsty savages. This war-decorated hero would have gladly turned in his medal and his pension for another tour in the service. Not because he loved the action, but because he would have had a purpose.

He is no different than every one of us. We all need to have a purpose in life in order to truly experience happiness. The problem is that many of us either don't clearly see our role in the world, or we don't see it at all. The most insidious thing about the latter one is that it can lead to depression and misery; slowly pulling you away from happiness. For me, the realization of my purpose came slowly, in increments. I knew from an early age that I was going to leave a mark on this earth that would shine like a beacon. That is the first part of the road to finding your purpose. You need to believe that you were created to do something that will forever change the lives of the people around you, if not the world.

And change them for the better.

I also feel that there is no true evil in this world, just misguided minds and souls who are desperately trying to find their purpose in life, their role. In order to come to the realization that you are more than

VIII. FINDING YOUR PURPOSE

just a pixel in a faceless crowd, you need to stop and think about who you really are, and what you really want. That is the first step. As soon as you begin to think about how you want to be remembered when you leave this earth, you are already on your way to becoming that person. It is the same principle Alcohol Anonymous uses. In order to stop drinking, you first need to realize that you have a drinking problem.

When you think about your legacy, your journey is at the hardest stretch of the road. In order to truly find a purpose in life, you need to learn about yourself, and devote time to continue questioning what your true desires are. This is where most of us struggle, as it is not a universal thing. Everyone has their own purpose, and the realization of it cannot be the same for everyone. I will tell you what I firmly believe my purpose in life is. For me, achieving business success was a big part of my purpose, but not the most important part. I strived to reach the top of my field and I managed to do it, but my legacy won't be the millions of dollars I leave to my children, or that I donate to charity. That is someone else's purpose and some of you will become that person. I would prefer leaving my kids with knowledge and passion that will teach them how to live a fulfilled life, something that will help them to achieve their own purpose and make their own fortunes rather than leaving them money and wealth. That is one of the reasons why I am writing this book. I know that God allowed the weight of tragedy that I experienced to prove to me that I am more than capable of carrying it. You are no different than I; trust me on that. Every one of us is capable of achieving greatness, whatever that might entail. It's not easy, it's not sudden, and it can change over time, but if you keep chasing it, and if you stay true to yourself, you are guaranteed to succeed.

I have always stayed true to my inner voice, and although there were some bumps along the way, I found what makes me happy and fought for it with every ounce of my strength.

I had the chance to speak to that hero soldier a while back. He now owns a gym where he trains war veterans who lost their limbs or who are physically disabled. He runs it the same way his staff sergeant ran it when he was first enlisted, and his business is booming; most importantly, he is happy. Not because he has a good business or because he attained financial wealth. He's happy because he now wakes up every day at 5:00 am knowing that there are dozens of people depending on him to push them through that day. He found his purpose in giving other people theirs. I did too, in my own way. When I stop to think about it, I realized that giving other people purpose is the precise reason why I love both of my careers. As a real estate broker, I get people into homes they like, that they want to center their lives in, therefore validating their desires, their road toward happiness. As a transformational coach, I do the same by enabling my clients to get a hold of their lives, get in shape, both physically and mentally, and gather the strength to keep marching down their life's path. The best part about helping people and coaching them to a better life is that as much as my clients benefit from the transformation, I am benefiting from it too, just as that soldier inspires his clients. With this book, I am sharing my experience, my life story, my views on meaning and purpose, hoping to help you find all those things for yourself.

I want you to think about your life as much as I did about mine. Try to learn about yourself as much as you can, and never stop doing it. This segment is called *Creating a Roadmap for a Better Life* and that's exactly what I'm hoping you will do. Earlier, I wrote that instincts are your guidelines in that roadmap. Well, the purpose is the scale. When you find your purpose in life, you know exactly what the scale of your life will be. It is like determining if you are building

VIII. FINDING YOUR PURPOSE

your fortress of solitude because that is what makes you happy, or if you are building a skyscraper filled with offices and people that work toward making your ideas come true and change people's lives. That scale matters, and as long as you keep comparing your true desires to the scale of the roadmap, you are doing it right. Following the roadmap that matches your honest desires prevents you from making mistakes. When you have the best intentions, mistakes are not backward steps, but sideways. Each mistake is only a lesson that you needed to learn in order to build your life from that roadmap.

I have not failed. I have just found 10,000 ways that won't work.

—— Thomas Edison

It is not something that I created, it's something that I adopted from others. One of the greatest conclusions that I have come to by myself is that when things get really hard, before asking others for help, I need to see if that is the kind of hardship that only I can overcome, that no one is actually more capable of dealing with it than me. You often hear people saying, "Asking for help is difficult." Well, there is truth in that statement, but I have a different view on it. It is hard to ask yourself for help. It is such a taboo thing these days that many people don't dare to admit to themselves that they need help. Once you realize that, it's not hard to ask others at all. It is natural, but you need to start with yourself.

I want to go back to the quote at the beginning of the chapter: "You do not attract what you want, you attract what you are." It is in this elegant quote that you realize your purpose in life. In order to get on the path toward a better life, if you do not act according to your inner voice, your purpose, your true desires, you can only get there by getting lucky. Counting on luck is not a life philosophy that you want to adopt. Luck is volatile and cruel, and it only leads to temporary gratification, rarely true happiness.

If I were to choose the message from this chapter that should resound in your mind the loudest, the message would say: *"keep questioning yourself until you find your purpose and then keep comparing your actions to it."* If they are in sync, you have nothing to worry about. It is only a matter of time and you are guaranteed to succeed. If they are not in sync, you are going to need to make some changes in your life. I honestly believe that you will realize what your next step should be on your own and it will be better than taking advice blindly. When it comes to purpose, no one but you will know with certainty what God has planned for you. You have the tools, you have the idea, and it is your responsibility to listen to your inner voice. When you start acting in accordance with it, the road signs on that journey will guide you toward a better life. Sounds easy when you think about it, right?

Chapter 8 – Exercise

Who are you, deep inside your soul?

1.

2.

Who do you want to be? Your deepest desires, your reason for being born.

1.

2.

3.

4.

5.

Are you following your "dharma"? Why you were created?

1.

2.

3.

4.

5.

Name 3 things you have overcome. Are you proud of it?

1.

2.

3.

If you do what you have always done, you will get what you have always gotten

-—— Tony Robbins

IX. CHALLENGING YOURSELF

"Dear Lord, let me win the lottery tonight, it would mean the world to me and my family, it would save us from the struggle we face every single day. I promise to say a prayer to you every day, just let me win tonight. The next week, the same man kneeled again and prayed for the same thing: *Dear Lord, you are almighty and all powerful, let me win the lottery tonight and I promise to make a good use of it. It would mean the world to me and my family, we are struggling every day. Please let me win tonight.* This went on for weeks until finally the man kneeled down and addressed God: *Dear Lord, why have you forsaken me? I prayed for weeks for just this one thing and you ignored me. I struggle so hard, we barely make ends meet. Why wouldn't you grant me this one thing I so desperately need?* As the man broke down in tears, he finally heard the voice: *So why don't you buy the ticket?"*

We are all creatures of habit, and more than anything, most of us hate change. Look at the way modern society is built. We build houses to permanently settle us at one location. Where that used to be beneficial 10,000 years ago because they had to live where there was food and water in abundance, it is completely different these days. Take Las Vegas for example, a city in the middle of the desert where nothing grows, where the sun scorches the ground, where less than 10,000 people lived just a 100 years ago. Now, it's built solely on entertainment and having fun, is home to more than 1.5 million people, and is visited by more than 40 million people every year. Settling down at a precise location was necessary decades ago, but nowadays it's not. However, we still live the old way because we don't like to change. That begs the question: *If you never change, what becomes of you in the future?* Many people are actually convinced that change is bad, and they are hoping that things will remain the same.

Change is neither good or bad—it's inevitable.

Look at my life, for example. When I was a younger, you had to be at home for someone to reach you by phone. If you wanted to see distant relatives from other continents, you would have to jet back and forward and meet them in person. Just a decade ago, if you wanted to send someone an SMS, you had to press the 9 four times just to get to the letter S. I'm typing this book on a computer that has 120 million times more computational power than the computers on-board the Apollo mission. If you were to ask me how the hell did I learn how any of the new technology works, I'd be damned if I knew how to answer that. Change is inevitable. The reason I am pointing in this direction is because it is the cornerstone of creating the roadmap for a better life. If you are looking to build a better life, you need to change the things that have prevented you from doing it so far. Once you figure out who you are right now, and who would you like to become, it's time to get to work and challenge yourself. Most of the good changes don't come cheap and you have to work for them and it's not going to come easy. This is true for all aspects of life: business, health, fitness, intellect, emotional, spiritual. Everything works on the same principle. You have to start making those small changes to keep getting closer to your destination.

IX. CHALLENGING YOURSELF

I met an endurance racer a couple of years back, and he had the most unique perspective on life and personal challenges. He runs ultra-marathons, and at the time we met, he was preparing for a 100-mile race. When I asked him what drives him to push himself that far out, he said, "I figure out life while I'm running." It made complete sense to me. From that short sentence I realized that I was just like him. All the stuff I challenge myself with helps me figure out who I really am, what I really want to achieve in my lifetime, and the impression I am going to leave on the people that I meet. When I decided to complete my education, I had not given thought as to why I wanted to be in the real estate business. Even though I wasn't aware of the reasons on an intellectual level, I knew them deep in my heart. I wasn't good at it in the beginning. Not even close. Then the housing market crashed in 2008, and even the best realtors struggled. Many of them left the industry back then, but I didn't. I kept hammering on and devised a plan. I challenged myself every single day and kept thinking about what I was doing wrong, constantly putting myself in those situations looking to figure out a solution. Some days it felt hopeless, but then I would improve just a tiny bit. I knew it was only a matter of time. If I kept challenging myself to learn new skills, new types of approaches, if I kept meeting people who are better at it than I am, I knew I was going to make it. Here I am—at the top 1% nationwide in the industry. It wasn't because I inherited a family business or because I had a good idea that no one thought of. It was because I worked tirelessly and kept improving, and I kept challenging myself to change for the better. It makes success that much sweeter and fulfilling.

I want to go back to this statement I stated earlier: *If you would ask me how the hell did I learn how any of the new technology works, I'd be damned if I knew how to answer that.* Actually, I know exactly how I learned it. Slowly, in increments, with great effort, despite the fact that it was hard. You are no different that I. I am not a wizard that figured out the secrets of the universe. I keep telling the people that I coach the same general idea. Fitness is the easiest area to use as an example. If you are trying to lose weight, you have to challenge yourself to eat healthier, stay active, and commit to it. One of my former clients was an IT expert and he struggled to keep his weight in check. That messed with his ability to earn a living. I asked him to tell me about his life and about his true passions. During these conversations I figured out that he was super-competitive and that he was an excellent chess player.

I challenged him to improve his rating by 5%. He called me a week later and said he did it. The first thing I told him was, "Step on the scale right now." He lost close to 4 pounds that week. I knew that if I could get him to focus on a challenge, his entire daily routine would change, and he would stay away from the junk food he was addicted to. He realized that the problem was in his approach. Whenever he would get stuck on a problem that needed serious mental investment in order to be solved, he would resort to eating foods that were bad for him. Instead of resorting to the old habit, the old way of thinking, when he got the urge to eat unhealthy foods, he would ask me to workout with him. We would run side by side, not saying a single word to each other. Then he would suddenly stop running, look at me, and say: "I got it, I know where I made the mistake." He would hug me and that was it.

He kept getting in better shape. During our final session, we ran for almost 11 miles, the furthest we have ever gone. I was exhausted and he seemed fresh. When I couldn't take it anymore, I stopped and asked him, "Is the problem that serious that you cannot figure it out?" He turned around and told me, "Not at all, I figured it out on the second mile marker. I just wanted to come up with a system that would prevent that problem from ever popping up again."

The good thing about challenging yourself is that you don't need my stories to validate it as the right approach. Think back to some of the stuff you have accomplished. What do you consider as one of your great achievements? Now think about how that came about? Were you good at it from the get go, or did you fail many times before you succeeded? When you challenged yourself at it, why did you do it?

That's the real beauty of human nature. We already have an innate understanding of life—we just need to apply it. There isn't a single person in the world that deep in their hearts doesn't know why they are struggling with a certain thing. You may not have the exact answer, but challenging yourself and exposing yourself to new ways of thinking and doing those things will crystallize the image and clearly reveal the exact nature of it. I struggled emotionally with David and, deep inside, I knew he wasn't the guy for me. We could have had a nice life together, but I would never have been as happy with him as I am with Viktor. If I never challenged myself to look for more, I would have never found Viktor. In fact, if I had never challenged myself to look for more, I would probably have been dead at the age of 15.

In order to change any aspect of your life for the better, you need to challenge yourself and get out of the comfort zone that prevents you from doing so. The problem is that many people think that the comfort zone, the status quo is a safety net, and this is what keeps them in a bubble. What I want you to think about is this: If you never try anything new, if you don't challenge yourself, that safety net will trap you because you can never get away from it. If you are unhappy with your life, why not strive for something bigger? If you fail, you either learned something about the problem, or you learned something about yourself. In many cases, it's both. You can always go back to doing what you were already doing, right? Nature shows us the best examples. If the bird never leaves the nest, how the hell is it ever going to fly? Yes, they can fall out of the nest and drop all the way to the ground, but it can't go any lower than that, and it can still try to fly again. In fact, in most cases, if it keeps trying it's only a matter of time before it happens. Many would argue that the ground is full of predators and that taking a risk rarely pays off.

If you are not happy, what is it that you are risking in the first place?

Here is a mental exercise I want you to do. As you read these questions, try to answer them as truthfully as you can. There is no point in lying to yourself, but then again, if you are at a point in your life where you are voluntarily reading my book, you probably are ready to commit to building a better life anyway. These questions are in the exercise at the end of the chapter. I encourage you to write them down as well.

What was the happiest moment of my life?

Is it associated with business, relationships, family, health, spirituality? Or is it a combination of these?

Do you want to go back to that place to experience that feeling again and again?

What's the main reason you cannot do that?

Is it in your power to address that reason? If not, is there a way to resolve the problem?

I want you to put a memo in your phone and ask yourself these questions tomorrow—and then the day after that, and the day after that. Repeat it until you have the clearest answers.

Since every one of us is on a different path, some of us will struggle with this for a while, some won't. Don't worry, that is completely normal. Heck, I sure hope that some of you will have all that stuff already figured out.

When you get to the point that most of these answers are clear to you, the path to the solution will start presenting itself. Even if it is just the first step, even if you don't see it clearly, don't hesitate to take it! This is what challenging yourself is all about. Keep putting yourself out there.

> *"If you put off everything until you're sure of it, you'll never get anything done."*
>
> — Norman Vincent Peale

When you complete a challenge, find another one, and then another one after that. Keep finding the challenges and you will start to get closer and closer to your ultimate goal. In the roadmap of the better life, instincts are the guidelines, and purpose is the scale. These challenges represent foundations for you to build that life on. These foundations, like any, require diligent work, overcoming obstacles on the terrain, and adapting to the circumstances. If done right, you can build a small cabin to live a cozy little life in, or you can build a skyscraper that will house your entire empire. That's the beauty of it. The same principles apply.

Chapter 9 – Exercise

1. What was the happiest moment of my life?

2. Is it associated with business, relationships, family, health, spirituality, or is it a combination of these?

3. Do you want to go back to that place to experience that feeling again and again? If not, What's the main reason you cannot do that? Is it in your power to address that reason? If not, is there a way to resolve the problem?

IX. CHALLENGING YOURSELF

4. Have you challenged yourself recently or have you become stuck in the day to day living with little or no happiness?

5. What can you do to change it? List three ways that you can change it starting today.

What you seek is seeking you

— Rumi

X. ATTACKING ANXIETY

Life brings about strange issues within ourselves. Some of these issues that we often think are caused by external factors actually exist only in our conscious mind and in our misguided thoughts. Anxiety is a great example of this. So many people do not have a clear understanding of what anxiety really is. I've had many clients that were suffering from severe anxiety attacks that doctors said were uncurable, without any idea how to combat it other than using medication of course. I have devised two ways of approaching anxiety and explaining it to my clients, and to everyone for that matter. There is a pure *logic and scientific approach*, and one I like using the most: *the animalistic approach*. I'll start with the first one.

Looking up the definition of anxiety will most often result in this particular phrasing: *a feeling of worry, nervousness, or unease about something with an uncertain outcome.* Focus all of your attention to the following three words from the definition: Feeling, Uncertain, Outcome.

Feeling

The feeling related to anxiety is basically in your head. Yes, you do feel the effects of anxiety in your stomach and it can make you sweat, or dizzy, or increase your heart rate, but the physical manifestation starts in your head. The feeling part is actually the conscious part of the brain over-thinking certain situations and scenarios and getting rattled. That results in the rest of your autonomous nervous system compensating and reacting to the fact that your thoughts are going in the wrong direction. Don't worry, this is quite normal, and it actually is a very useful part of our entire personality mechanism. The same principles apply when you visualize stuff beforehand, like striking a perfect drive in golf. The conscious part of your brain actually prepares the movement and readies your body for the act itself. When people say, "I feel the shot," this is, in fact, what that is. This means if you master the art of visualization, you will actually perform the set act more efficiently and with a greater rate of success. The same goes for anxiety. It starts in your head and it puts you in a state of fear, aggressiveness, or frailty, and your body follows. That's the catch—it's a feeling that starts in your head, which means you have the ability to control it—you just need to master it.

Uncertain

This is another ludacris and somewhat inexplicable mechanism that makes anxiety self-treatable. The uncertainty element means that we do not know whether it is *good or bad*, but yet we calculate only the *bad* things in the case of anxiety. Just like the previous element, this is also completely normal. Take learning how to ride a bike, for example. When you first sat on the bike, it was uncertain whether you would fall and perhaps scrape your knee, or you would continue riding on. The desire to figure it out broke the uncertainty barrier and you learned how to ride. Now there was still uncertainty in the outcome every time you sat on that bike, and it is present today as much as it was that first time. You trained your brain to calculate more positive than negative results, and now you don't feel uncomfortable when take a bike ride. The same technique can be used for anxiety. Uncertainty literally means that you cannot determine the ratio of *good vs bad* outcomes, so training your conscious mind not to immediately pile on the bad thoughts is quite possible, and I will explain these techniques shortly.

Outcome

This word basically tells us that the thing we obsess and worry about, the thing that makes us anxious has not even happened yet. We are yet to see or experience the events that cause us to feel anxious right now. Stop and read that sentence again. Do you see how strange that sounds? That is a normal thing and we use that conscious mechanism almost daily. For example, when you drive and see a red light 200 yards down the road, you know a car in front of you is about to slow down. It hasn't happened yet, but you can plan ahead for it and you do it automatically. Now the thing is, you don't give any thoughts to the car behind you because you cannot control and predict those events. That's anxiety—worrying about the car behind you that you have no control over. Yes, you can flash your lights, try to draw their attention, hoping that they will notice you and slow down as well. Ultimately, should you be doing that every time you stop at the red light? So, why do you do that during anxiety attacks? Why are you trying to figure out and control events that are yet to happen and that you probably cannot affect?

Here is another way of explaining it. This is the animalistic one that makes so much sense to me. Imagine an impala grazing the grass in the middle of the African savanna. Its instincts are telling it two things: *there are predators around, but you need to eat in order to stay alive because there is a chance there won't be grass fields for another 15 miles ahead, or ever again for that matter.* Now, it needs to be said that an impala is not a conscious being with a highly developed sense of identity like most of us are. We really ought to learn from the animal kingdom a lot more. That impala will always stop and graze the field. It will stay cautious, but it won't get anxious. It takes all the precautionary measures, watches the entire field around it looking for signs of the predators, but its heart rate is not increased, it is not distressed by any means, and it is not in agony. So there are no bad feelings, no uncertainty, and no outcome yet. It's living in the present. When a lioness starts running, and ONLY when a lioness starts running toward it, then the flight-or-fight mechanism triggers and the impala acts accordingly. Do you see the difference? This gracious animal is cautious, and it is prepared for both good and bad outcomes, but it doesn't stress over the uncertain events until they actually happen.

I want you to be an impala.

I want you to awaken the animal within you and learn to control those feelings that cause you real physical distress. I want you to train your body and your mind to deal with real and perceived threats. Imagine if an animal goes through life fearing every single threat that lurks? It would starve within days.

Let me tell you why this is an important subject and how it is applicable in your everyday life. The daily struggles we endure in this modern society are de-facto, pulling us in the opposite direction of our primal urges which are to fight, to love, to explore, to achieve. That is the burden of the daily grind most of us experience. So from the get go, achieving any type of success is an uphill battle. Now you have to factor in your true desires and goals, and the difficult task of getting to the bottom of that barrel and figuring it out. That puts another couple of degrees on the gradient. If you allow anxiety to grab a hold of you, that only means that the already-difficult terrain that you are building your life on is constantly shifting that gradient. It's like trying to build a solid structure on a tilted table that doesn't actually react to the load you put on it. No, this table reacts to all potential loads you might ever put on it. Who can balance a table like that? What kind of a structure can you build on it?

Over the years of battling with my own anxiety and talking to people that have similar issues, I tried many techniques and listened to loads of advice. What I ultimately figured out was that it is up to me, and me alone to deal with it and figure it out. Even if you see a professional and seek help that way, do you know what that help entails? Asking questions. That's what professionals that deal with anxiety do most of the time—and it works. They ask questions you don't think of asking yourself. They teach you to attack and battle your anxiety by demystifying it at its core. I wouldn't go as far as to suggest not seeing a specialist when you suffer from anxiety attacks, but I think that you should try to figure it out on your own first. Ask yourself questions when you feel most distressed, try and figure out what the hell is going on.

Here is what I would like you to do the next time you experience an anxiety attack. First, breathe. Slowly, deeply, in and out. Take a minute or two and focus just on the movement, belly outwards on the inhale, inwards on the exhale, in and out. Then start paying attention to your surroundings:

Where are you?

What are you doing?

Are you in any immediate danger?

Look for familiar cues that can harbor your conscious thought. If you are not in any immediate danger, there is no need for your heart rate to be elevated. As the title suggests, *If you Seek for Calm, the Calm Seeks for You*. Realizing that the problems that are causing the anxiety to have not occurred yet will make you calmer.

Start weighing up the likelihood of the positive and negative outcomes you are expecting, but use logic at the same time. The negatives you can counter with positives should no longer be a part of that equation. Finally, try to figure out what caused that feeling in the first place and how you can better be prepared so that it doesn't happen again. Most of the time, it is the fear of failure that causes anxiety attacks, but we already know that failing is great. In fact, the next chapter will focus solely on that fact—failing is great. Anxiety is the tilt table that can, as it shifts, turn your thoughts in the wrong direction and mess up your compass. It is a storm that will cloud your skies and capsize your boat, confuse your sense of direction, and send you where you don't want to go. Always remember, if you stay afloat when the storm passes, you can always figure out where the east is when the sun rises. That is the thing that pushes me through every anxiety attack I experience. Regardless of the severity, the realization that I am getting overly worked up about events that haven't happened yet, that are still to be determined in terms of being good or bad, and lastly, that the feeling is in my head, not in my bones and body, helps me to overcome it. You can learn how to do that as well.

The time invested focusing on that kind of a personal growth will prove its worth many times over. Every anxiety attack that you successfully disarm and get under control will increase the stability of the platform you are building the better life on. If you really feel like you cannot handle it on your own, seek help, and the help will seek you.

Chapter 10 – Exercise

1. Do you believe what you are seeking is seeking you? Why?

2. Think of your goals and your destiny, then list three ways you can execute your plan and start living the life you desire.

    a.

    b.

    c.

4. Reflect for a moment about a risk you faced at one time in your life. What fears or other emotions were present as you studied the risk?

5. What either prevented you from moving forward or propelled you to act despite the risk?

6. What did you learn about yourself through all of it?

Failure is simply the opportunity to begin again, this time more intelligentl

— Henry Ford

XI. FAILING IS GREAT

- Microwave oven
- Ink-jet printer
- Penicillin
- Potato chips
- Chocolate chip cookies
- Cornflakes
- Pacemakers
- X-Ray images
- Artificial sweetener
- Vulcanized rubber
- Teflon
- Safety glass

I am not much for the numbers game and statistics because they are often a subject of interpretation and the conclusions can portray a false image. For example, if a 70-year-old and a 10-year-old walk down the street, a statistician could argue that on average, they are two 40-year-olds which makes no sense. That is the reason why I usually don't quote numbers and percentages unless they can unequivocally prove a point. Here is a number that struck me—600,000. That's how many people each year have had their lives saved by getting a pacemaker. I was baffled by the number when I first read about it, but not as much as when I found out that the discovery of a pacemaker was actually an accident, a mistake. Likewise, penicillin was also a happy mistake. Antibiotics saved millions of lives (there is no actual number, just estimates, and some go as high as 200 million), and it was discovered as a byproduct of mistakes and lucky coincidences. In fact, go back to the top of the page and take a look at the list. Those were all invented by people failing at their primary goal. How many things from it are an integral part of your life? In fact, stop and consider how much of everything you are is owed to mistakes? I'll give you a hint: a statistician would call "a lot" a safe bet.

There is a point in all of this I want you to consider. It's not convoluted, it's not sophisticated, heck, it's not even mysterious and many people are aware of it. The point is this: *if you have never failed, you have never even tried*. It's as simple as that.

I used to have a *state of mind, state of body* practice with my clients back in the day. Whenever I met a new client, I tried to ascertain their limits, or should I better say their image of those limits. One hundred pushups was usually the number. I would ask them if they can do one hundred pushups. All of them would say NO. In caps, a resounding no. Some even tried to argue with me that they would never be able to do it because of their *bad physique, imaginary injuries* or some other excuse that they would use as a crutch to justify their lack of success. After letting them finish trying to convince me that it was something that was not feasible for them, I would ask, "When was the last time you tried? Have you ever tried to do it all? How come you know you can't do it then?" I would have them try to do it, and they would fail, over and over again. After 8. After 12. After 21. After 43. After 79. I had a 54-year-old woman who gave up after 94 completed pushups. For weeks they would fail. Most of them eventually reached

100. That lady did too. By the time they were fit enough to do it, they also figured out the underlying lesson:

Failure is not the opposite of success. It's a part of Success!

— Arianna Huffington

It's in the simple process of failing that you actually learn how to do things. Even if you never succeed in accomplishing what you have set out as a goal, you will still accomplish a lot of great things, and at the same time learn more about yourself and make great strides toward a happy life. I am fully aware that sometimes it is hard to recognize the lesson in the fail, but trust me, it's always there. When you look past the pain and the disappointment of failing, you will find the underlying point that will make you smarter, stronger, and more resilient. Embracing that point will enable you to go past the failure and get further. I heard a quote that if you really learned a lesson, you won't make the same mistake again. I don't believe that to be the case. Sometimes, things happen that are out of your control and that cause you to fail. You have to take that into account as well and embrace it. This is especially true when you set out to achieve something that cannot be touched, like happiness in a relationship. Many relationships fail and they do so for all sorts of reasons. When you experience such a fail, you have to look past it and really be honest with yourself. Perhaps you failed in it, perhaps you didn't, but the outcome wasn't positive. You have to face the reality that not many people find their soulmate the first time round, and it may take you several times before you succeed. It can hurt, it can be tiring, but consider the alternative. If you are afraid of failure, you won't bother trying, and that will leave you feeling even worse. Regret will hurt a lot more down the line, and it will hurt forever.

I was blessed with many failures in life, and I do say blessed on purpose. I failed my real estate license exam the first time. I failed in many relationships before I met Viktor. I am probably failing right now with this entire book. None of it is actually a bad thing because maybe this book won't help a lot of you, or it won't help you a lot, or it won't change your view of the life and make it better from the core. It might, though! If it fails, but some of you really find it inspiring and helpful, I will take that as a lesson: the messages I tried to send to the world was good, I just chose the wrong words. When I do run out of the words to shape my thoughts in the proper way, I can always find them in someone else's quotes.

> *Success is the ability to go from one failure to another with no loss of enthusiasm.*
>
> — Winston Churchill

This quote resonates a lot with me because it was said by a person who was convinced of it. During World War II, Sir Winston Churchill employed a person named Alan Turing. He was a mathematician who was convinced that he could break the Enigma machine used by German troops to communicate with their ranks. His idea was to design a machine that would do the work for them. Everyone in the military was against the idea, but Churchill allowed him to do it. This machine failed time and time again, but Alan Turing would not give up and he was sure that each mistake was bringing him closer to solving it. Churchill believed him, and while the rest of the commanding staff were pushing for the project to be shut down, they prevailed. Eventually, the team Alan assembled managed to break the Enigma code and decipher the messages shortening the war considerably. The mistakes that Alan made in this process made him think way outside the box and think of a machine that would be able to solve any problem. He laid the foundations of modern computing and AI. In fact, without him

XI. FAILING IS GREAT

failing, the world would be a much different place. Now imagine if he gave up after the third time he failed? Or after the 33rd. Or even after the 433rd? He was facing approximately 158 million million million to one chance of breaking it. He knew that each mistake figuratively, and sometimes literally, took a zero off of that number. He succeeded.

What I am trying point out using this example is that you should never be afraid of the odds that are stacked against you and failing to beat them. You should only be afraid of giving up early or not trying at all.

No matter how many mistakes you make or how slow you progress, you are still way ahead of everyone who isn't trying.

— Tony Robbins

I want you to try taking a different approach to your view of the fails you've made. Instead of focusing on the fact that you failed, focus on the steps after it. Embrace the defeat and try to deduce what went wrong. Was it something you could have predicted, and why didn't you? Was it in your control or outside of it? What can you do better next time? Take time to re-evaluate the goal you tried to accomplish with that last try. If that goal still seems desirable and attainable, gather your strength back, and go after it again. Hope for the success, plan for other outcomes.

There is a professor of electrical engineering that used to come to my lectures and I would often mention him. The first time I spoke about failing and the importance of it, he waited for me after the lecture and explained a method that he is using in the classroom. He taught the basics of electrical engineering as a hobby to kids from broken homes. He wanted them to attain the skills that would serve them for the rest of their lives. One of the first lessons he would give them was the *shock lesson*. While studying soldering, he would tell them to solder a live wire, without teaching them to check it first. The wire was hooked to a 9-volt battery which then shocked them as soon as they touch it. The strength of the shock was minuscule, it wouldn't hurt a fly, but the surprise was real, and very impactful. None of them repeated the same mistake again. He knew that in order to really understand how important that lesson was, they had to fail at it first. By his records, more than 400 of his students are now successful electrical engineers and repairman, and many of them bring the kids on their own for him to teach them the same lessons.

The reason I mention him in my lectures is that he made me realize some mistakes simply have to happen. You cannot prevent them, or better said, you shouldn't even try to prevent them because the lessons those mistakes teach are far more valuable than any discomfort you endure making it. Thinking back and applying the same reasoning to the situations in my life made me at peace with some of the mistakes I made that haunted me for quite a while. I am sure that you will experience the same relief if you apply it to your previous experiences as well. That's why I called this chapter *Failing is great*, because deep down in its essence, it really is. It's not always beautiful, it's not always pleasant, it can hurt at times, but it is always meaningful. Try to find the meaning in it and even if you cannot, you will find some other pieces of the puzzle that perhaps you don't know where they belong right now, but in the bigger picture, they will fit perfectly somewhere in your life. I have one last quote in this chapter for you guys:

Keep in mind that neither success nor failure is ever final.

— Roger Babson

Chapter 11 – Exercise

What are at least three things you have failed at?

What did you learn from the failure?

Did it show you how to do it differently?

Has it given you more strength, knowledge and gumption?

Success is doing what you want, when you want, where you want, with whom you want, as much as you want

— Tony Robbins

XII. DESIRING MORE OUT OF LIFE

There was a prayer that I used to say every night in the moments of pure solitude: *God, please allow me to dream big, give me the strength to work toward achieving those dreams and perseverance to chase them despite the odds stacked against me.* I don't say that prayer anymore for the simple reason that the prayer has been answered. Thinking back, I shouldn't have put that on God. I figured out that there are things you don't need to ask from anyone, things no one should give you because you can do them on your own. Imagine if each and every one of us would ask God for the things we already have, or are able to acquire on our own. The true gratitude would disappear and all the prayers would be de facto useless. What I am praying for these days is for God's blessing to provide me with the peace of mind that I am doing the right thing. My prayers are granted each and every day. I am forever grateful to the Almighty because without Him, without the words He ever so softly whispers in my ears when I really struggle, I wouldn't be anywhere near the place I am today. I wouldn't say I owe my success to God directly, only by proxy. That's because it wasn't God who gifted me with a great life. I, the same way as you are all capable of too, earned and built it myself, with the help of my family. It was me who worked tirelessly, constantly overcoming any and all obstacles on my path. God gave me exactly what I asked for: the peace of mind. The greatest gift you could and should ever hope to receive from God is His guiding hand. No one can do the work for you. You have to build your life for yourself. In order to do that, you have to desire more out of life.

What exactly does *desiring more out of life* mean? Well, that's unique and different for all of us. Moreover, it constantly changes. One of the most common reasons why people have an unhappy life is that they are stuck in a dead end job that crushes their soul. I am quite certain that many of you feel like, or at some point felt like, life is passing you by while you slave away at a nine to five doing something you hate. I've had those same feelings for a good part of my life, working all sorts of jobs, just to keep a roof above my head and the heads of my family. Before Charles died, I was either too lazy or too scared to act on it. I fell into a routine and I always figured there would be time to turn my life around. His death was the trigger for me, and I started acting on my desires. Thinking back, it wasn't as much a necessity that the situation required, being a widow at 24 with two kids and no job skills, it was my determination to finally act on my desires, and it took something monumental to turn my life around. As much as I thought I needed a miracle or a sign from God, it wasn't the case. It isn't the case for you either.

You don't need monumental events to turn your life around.

It wasn't until I met Viktor and we spent one of those first nights talking about life in general that I realized it. In a moment of pure and brutal honesty, I admitted to myself that I could have made the change while Charles was alive. I had the will, but I just wasn't at peace with it and didn't have a crystal clear vision about what my true desires were. Once I figured it out, I was determined and started taking steps toward making it happen. So the things I actually needed from God wasn't the strength or the perseverance. I have that, you have it too, whether you are aware of it or not. This quote sums it up perfectly.

XII. DESIRING MORE OUT OF LIFE

Begin to live as though your prayers are already answered.

— Tony Robbins

I started working hard, trying to edge my way, just a step closer to what my desires were. My life is a testament of this method: every failure is a step in the right direction, every success is a leap toward your goals. Once I achieved a certain goal, I basked in the glory and it felt good, like nothing you could experience otherwise—but only for a while, because of that win, that success fueled me immensely and I started to believe there was more for me out there—and there was. There still is. Up until this day, I've achieved a lot: business-wise, in my personal growth, with a happy family. Some things I devoted my time to have peaked and it joys me to say that I've reached the highest of limits imaginable. In other areas, I can still grow.

That's what makes me happy.

I am proud of the things I have achieved, but motivated to grow even more in the areas where I feel like there is room for me to do so. For example, this book is all about that. I enjoy my success, but at the same time there is this something that drives me to share my story and allow other people to learn from my mistakes, to recognize their own potential. For me, that means desiring more out of life. For you, it could be getting that degree from the college you dropped out of, getting that promotion, starting your own business, turning your social life around, or it could be as simple as finding peace and clarity within the life you've already built.

Doing what you love is the cornerstone of having an abundant life.

— Wayne Dyer

Whatever that is, keep searching for it because the search itself is rewarding. If you have already found it, keep building it and share it with the people you love. The only thing you need to know up front is that sometimes, it won't be easy. In fact, for me, it wasn't easy at all. These hardships will put you to the test, and if you give up on desiring more, there is no outcome where you will be happy for the rest of your life. You can live a comfortable life, but true happiness requires constant challenges. I used to consider that a bit paradoxical, but during a lecture I attended several years back summed it up perfectly. The lecture was not about success, not about business, not about recipes for a happy life. It was about the basics of human nature.

When humans first developed conscious thought, when we started having our own sense of identity, we weren't living in cities, and we weren't permanently settled in just one place with everything at our disposal. We were hunter-gatherers, which means no matter who you were, what you achieved yesterday, you still needed to provide the food for today. That means you had to overcome the challenge of catching an animal or finding anything edible in the vicinity. That wasn't an easy task at all. Deep in our nature, there is a primal voice that constantly looks for challenges. This voice used to be a lot stronger because we depended on it all the time in order to survive. Nowadays, we try to shut it up, to mute it, because it's convenient.

That's a mistake.

If you don't feed your true desires, they grow weak and weary. If you don't give voice to them, if you don't devote any time nurturing those instincts, you cannot attain true happiness. My advice is to let the animal within you speak its mind. Try to listen, to understand, align your life as much as possible with those ideas and you will start to turn those desires into something more and get the best out of life.

XII. DESIRING MORE OUT OF LIFE

There are several things that stand in the way of those desires and living a happy life. I, with a great degree of certainty, claim that fear and laziness are probably the biggest issues for most of us. We are afraid of taking chances, especially if our situation is somewhat manageable as it is. We compromise and lower our standards just because we are scared to fail, or are too lazy to really work on our dreams. Those exact things suffocate the very essence of our identity and soul. I was guilty of it, and in those moments, I would pray to God to give me that strength; but I wasn't lacking strength, I just lacked a clear vision, a clear goal.

I recently spoke about it during a coaching session with a client. I wanted her to realize that the journey to a better life started within her. So I told her to imagine being an archer. Archery requires a lot of training and dedication, a lot of upper body strength, all of which you can achieve without ever picking up a bow. No matter how strong your hands are, no matter your composure, the chances of you striking a target on your first try are miniscule. So instead of building up strength, instead of doing it blindly without a target in sight, why not try a different approach? Find a target first and try to hit it. You will miss just the same, but the next arrow will come closer to that bull's eye. Some arrows will be closer than others, but the more you shoot at it, the stronger your hands will be, the closer your arrows will come. Eventually, you will be able to hit it on every time. But the work is not over. Oh no. Hitting it every time will feel good for a while, and then it won't. What you want to do is step ten feet back and try it again. Once you master that, move ten feet back again. Doing that, one of two things will happen: either you will reach incredible distance and make yourself truly great, a world famous archer with all the accolades that go with it, or you will find your limit and have the satisfaction that you mastered something and conquered your laziness, your fears, your doubts. In both cases, you will feel great, and not just temporarily. You will feel great for the rest of your life. In both cases, you will find new challenges in passing your knowledge to others, sharing your experience, teaching others to break your records, and reliving that thrilling path and each of those successful stages all over again.

When you stay on purpose and refuse to be discouraged by fear, you align with the infinite self, in which all possibilities exist.

— Wayne Dyer

It is tricky to make yourself desire more out of life, but for those of you who commit to it, the journey itself will be just as rewarding as the destination. That's what living is all about. Don't live for the couple of fleeting moments that will come later. Live each moment like you are already there, and the journey will be just as memorable and just as rewarding.

Chapter 12 – Exercise

1. Are you doing something every single day that you love? It can be a walk in nature, reading a book, volunteering, Taking your kids to the park, having tea with a friend or doing something you are passionate about? It does not have to be big.

2. What would happen if you did three things every day that you love?

3. What is your biggest fear? Bungee jumping, flying, speaking to a crowd?

4. Are you willing to face your fear and break out of the old habits that have kept you from living the life you desire?

5. Are you scared of what will happen if you follow your desire? What will happen if you don't?

YOU ARE IN CHARGE OF YOUR LIFE

XIII. USING THE KNOWLEDGE AROUND YOU

I've been known for having a firm belief in what I'm saying and especially in what I'm doing. It's not just an opinion I have about it, countless people told me that I honestly seem genuine. In fact, anytime I have a conversation with anyone, that's one of the most likely impressions I leave on a person. This is because I don't usually jibber jabber just to sound smart or to have my voice heard. I learned a long time ago that *thinking before you speak* is one of the most important traits a person can have. The great thing about acting like that is that you will never be a dumb person. Let me explain this using an example.

When I was starting out in my real estate career, a senior colleague of mine asked me out for lunch. He was a seasoned salesman and one of the people I looked up to in the business. He taught me so many things. When I say taught, it's not like he was my mentor or anything, it's just that he was willing to talk to me when no one in the business was. There used to be this weird competitive thing among sales personnel in general, and real estate business was one of the most competitive fields that showcased it. This gentleman was one of the best agents in the state at the time and he was a bit stubborn, often known for being eccentric at times. Well, having results like he did, no one took it as a flaw and many actually tried to emulate his style. We met for a lunch on several occasions, but I will never forget one of the conversations we had because it changed the course of my life. We sat and talked about marketing strategies and he was firmly committed to the opinion that home buyers are usually oblivious and that if you do your job right, they will believe every single thing you tell them. He even went as far as comparing his clients to sheep, and compared himself to Jesus. He went on a bit of a rant about it actually, which lasted for about 5 minutes.

 I sat there, a bit confused, and while he made a few good points, I didn't like his overall point of view. There was the moment when I could have agreed with him; he even wanted us to become business partners (that was actually the point of the lunch in question). I would have been a complete fool if I did. Instead, I sat there quietly thinking about what he just said. After about 5 minutes or so, I said, "Well, you have a certain strategy and based on your previous records, I believe that it produces some results. But, doesn't that leave you without the option for repeat business from your clients?" He sat there stunned, completely caught off-guard by my remark. After about 10 seconds he started trying to convince me that his point of view was 100% effective, and that his results proved that he was doing the right thing. He even started shouting a bit. I didn't mind. Here was the person whose entire essence was just questioned by a woman half of his age that clearly "knows nothing about the business". During his entire rant, I remember thinking, *why is he so passionate about this?* I didn't mean anything by it, I just honestly believe that your clients are your livelihood and the better service you provide, the better you treat them, the better your results will be. Then at one point, he slammed his hand on the table which kind of threw everyone at the restaurant off. He took a sip of water and sat there quietly for about a minute. Then he said, "You could be right." He told me that during his 30+ years in the business, he had never sold a house to the same client twice. We continued talking about the business and actually ended up talking for hours.

The reason I specifically remember this conversation is not because I learned the best secrets of the real estate business during that lunch. In fact, I didn't pick up new marketing strategies and I wasn't given any advice of sorts. I don't even remember what we specifically talked about after that situation. Instead, I learned that you should always search for new wisdom. At that particular moment I saw his brilliance. His entire career, which was massive compared to mine and most of the agents in the country, had only one type of approach. It worked for him. He heard my remark, he respected my courage to say it to his face, to challenge him on it, and he listened. I realized that then and there that this was why he was the best in the business. It wasn't a legacy, it wasn't the approach or the image, it wasn't even the *work more than all other agents'* philosophy. It was his ability to use all the available data surrounding him. Even though he reacted the way he did, it took him less than 5 minutes to figure out that what I was saying could be beneficial to him. That was an eye-opener for me. That's when I really started to realize this: seeking out new ideas and new perspectives is one of the most important business philosophies, and it's the practice I have continued to use to this date. Years later, just before he retired, he told me, "You will make it in this business. But you would be a fool to stop there. You have the ability to make it in whatever sphere of life you imagine. Never forget it." Every time I hit an obstacle, I remember his words. I want you to remember them as well.

That was years ago, but I just recently figured out that even before that took place, actually ever since I was old enough to think about anything, way before I thought about real estate, I knew that learning and improving are the best ways to overcome big obstacles in life. You just have to fuel those with the desire to make your life better, to achieve and strive for better things and better relationships, to genuinely work on your problems and see them as the steps on the ladder, not insurmountable stop signs that prevent you from rising above them.

I am proud to admit that a huge influence on me were people that broke the ground regarding self-improvement and self-help. The likes of Wayne Dyer, Tony Robbins, Earl Nightingale, Bob Proctor, Norman Vincent Peale, etc., whose books I've read multiple times, whose seminars I've attended, whose teachings helped me model my own life philosophy. Those are the people that I am thankful for. Each one of them has a different understanding of life and the importance of realizing what your true potential is, but they all sort of have the same idea behind it:

You have to be honest with yourself in order to achieve progress.

Ever since Charles died, I've been pretty honest with myself, regardless of how difficult it has been. I could have said, "Two kids won't leave me enough time to work on improving my skills, to attend classes, to build a business." I didn't. Instead, I had my own agenda and I wasn't fully aware of how to put it into words until just recently:

Making excuses is what makes them real. Stop making them, and they will stop hindering your progress.

— Romi Hancock

One of the most frequently-used excuses we use in everyday life are "*I don't know how to do that*" and "*I never did it and it's a bit late for me to start to.*" We use different wording or a slightly

XIII. USING THE KNOWLEDGE AROUND YOU 141

changed focus, but the base of these excuses is pretty much close to one or the other. I already gave you an answer that changes the perspective for the first excuse: *I don't know how to do that*. Did you try? How hard did you try? Did you give up on the first attempt? Also, try asking yourself a couple of things whenever you use that excuse: Did I forget how to learn new stuff? Or am I just lazy? Or is it that I am scared of not making it on the first attempt, so I don't even bother? These questions are so simple to answer, but you have to be honest with yourself and accept the answers as your current reality, not a permanent fixture. I'll give you an example.

When I moved back to Vegas, I was committed to re-building my business from scratch. I was happy about my effort for months. During that time, I wasn't reading much or keeping in the loop with current news. There was this moment I remember that again changed my life for the better. I was watching a game show, something similar to that Smarter Than a 5th Grader show, or it could have been that actual show, I'm not sure; but I remember the question: "What is the capital of Sweden?" I was dumbfounded. There I was, thoroughly aggravated for not knowing a geography question that a kid from elementary school aced on the first try. It wasn't the fact that I didn't know the answer, it was my entire mindset about feeling the thirst for knowledge, but not acting on it, because I was actually curious about the answer. *Why haven't I ever bothered to look it up?* I was fully aware that we are living in a time where such information doesn't require a visit to the library or owning an encyclopedia just typing a few words into a web search. That didn't help me settle down. I stayed awake for hours obsessing about it until, finally, I realized something. It is my current reality. I can change it whenever I want to. In fact, I will change it first thing in the morning. The next morning on my way to work, I didn't listen to music, I instead listened to an audiobook about Sweden, and on my way back, about Norway.

The following morning, about yoga. I changed my reality simply by acting on the obvious problem. I may not know what the capital of Cambodia is today, but you can rest assured that I will know it tomorrow, or the day after that. That's the whole point of this chapter. Use the knowledge around you.

If you have made it so far reading through my book, you probably already know that I often quote other people that I consider to be way smarter than I am. My aim is not to simply rehash their lessons. Their wisdom is my commodity and I use it to create and model my own life and help others do the same. Like I said before, if this book helps just one person and fuels them to turn their life around for the better, it will make it a success in my eyes. It will also prove that using the knowledge around you is a thing you should pay attention to.

Going back to that other excuse I mentioned: *I never did it and it's a bit late for me to start to.* We are a perfect generation to disprove this one. I was born at a time when this book would have been typed on a typewriter that uses physical force and an ink strip. A time when you had to be at home for someone to reach you by phone. When you had to wait for the relative from another continent to fly in just to see his face. In ten years, in ten short years, all that has changed. What if I had said when someone first asked me to use a smartphone, "I have never used one and it's a bit late for me to start now"? What if when online flight ticketing became a thing that I said the same? Do you see where I'm going with this? Things change, and they actually change significantly faster nowadays. You do change with them, whether you admit it to yourself or not. Why then would you ever think it is too late for you to start picking up new things?

I had a conversation with a lovely lady at an honorary gala for war veterans. Her late husband was one of the few who survived the storming of Omaha beach during WWII. We talked for about 15 minutes, and as she was about to walk away, she dropped her bag and from it, a French-English dictionary popped out. I asked if she knew how to speak French and she said, "Not yet, but one of these days." She noticed the confused look on my face and proceeded to tell me that her husband spent almost an entire year stationed in France after the end of the war, and that he learned how to make a specific pastry with sweet cheese. Ever since he died, she had been longing for it. So this lady, with all of her 89 years and glasses as thick as a honeypot, went online and looked up the name of the bakery her husband talked about. She found out that it was still open. So this extraordinary lady bought a French-English dictionary and she started learning the basics of it just so that she can go to France and taste the sweet cheese pastry once again. I cried my heart out right in front of her. She kept looking at me with the same smirk on her face, "Don't worry, I might even find me a lover there, if I find a fella looking like my Peter".

Such an unlikely place, from a complete stranger, I re-learned a lesson I already knew. There is no *too late* when it comes to doing new stuff. Moving to Vegas was sort of a similar thing for me because I knew it wasn't too late for me to start over and start looking for my soulmate. This sweet old lady reminded me of something I already knew. I am trying to do the same. I want you to keep reminding yourself that you are capable of change, capable of acquiring new skills and new knowledge, and that if you really open your eyes and open your soul, you will find the strength and the tools to make your life better.

> *Success is waking up every morning with an intention of being a better version of yourself and lying every night with the realization that tomorrow, you can do better.*
>
> — Romi Hancock

Chapter 13 – Exercise

1. Are you scared of change? You will need to dig deep inside to pull out this question inside you.

2. Have you ever considered living in a different city, state or country?

3. Have you considered a career change?

4. What would that look like?

XIV. INVEST IN YOURSELF

We live in the strangest times known to mankind. Never has there been a time where so much change and acceleration has been present as it has during the last 30 years. Just think about it. I recently found an old videotape that was labeled *Barbecue, spring 1998.* I couldn't watch it. Not because I am emotional or anything. I literally couldn't watch it because I had no device to put the tape in. Just think about it. In less than 20 years, technology essential to recording memories, technology so widespread, with no alternatives became completely obsolete. I already mentioned devices like the typewriter, landline phones, film cameras, etc. We can add many things to that list, including GSM pagers, Walkmans, Discmans mp3 players, calculators, floppy disks, and PDAs. Here is another example. Blockbuster was one of the biggest companies in the USA just a mere 15 years ago, but nowadays has less than a dozen stores. The point I am trying to make is that things are changing at a staggering pace and that makes it a very strange and difficult period of time to live in.

What then happens to us, in these strange times? To me? To our kids? To our parents and grandparents? Try to contemplate that for a minute. The kids who will be born this year, jobs that they will be doing are yet to be invented. It used to be like this: my dad was a blacksmith, his dad and grand-dad were blacksmiths, I am, and my kids will also continue the tradition. Well, that almost never happens anymore.

Probably not many of you thought about it in such a way, but it is a strike against our own nature. As the new things keep coming faster and faster, how do we keep up with them? How do we stay connected to ourselves and to the people that we love, and reconcile it all when it takes less than a decade for everything around you to change?

Invest in yourself. I do not mean like *spend money and buy yourself a bunch of stuff*. I am saying just the opposite. Do not spend the bulk of your money on stuff. Do not spend most of your time on pure indulgence, because that stuff is only temporary. These strange times have such a strong effect on all of us. We are now closer to each other than ever and yet there is more solace and loneliness among us which is widely noticeable and measurable. So what exactly do I mean by *invest in yourself?* It is simple. Keep working on getting to know the deep crevices of your soul and fill your life with experiences, not things. There is this great thing that any parent can confirm as an absolute truth. Children are innocent in a sense that their mind is pure. They don't know about anything malicious or impure. They cannot fathom a world where you are alienated from people. This is so for one simple reason: they are curious and the only motivation in their lives is quenching that thirst for knowledge, for experiences, for the love of the people, all people. This can also be confirmed by any parent in the world. There is this period in a child's life where you begin to see a semblance of their personality, a glimpse of the conscious thought trying to figure the world out. Kids have this amazing ability to sum it up in a single word: *Why?* Whatever you do, whatever you say, a child will ask you *why?* They do this because they want to know the motivation behind your actions. So how come we stop questioning them as we get older?

If you cannot explain your choices to a 5-year-old, you should question the motives behind those choices.

XIV. INVEST IN YOURSELF

— Romi Hancock

Everything you do in life is governed by some kind of motivation. When you eat, you want to persevere, when you have kids, you want to procreate and extend your genetic material, etc. You are, like every other organism on the planet, born with it. Have you ever considered greed? Have you ever considered the lust for power? These are motivating factors that many of us act on, a lot. You couldn't possibly be born with it, right? Well, as it turns out, you are. We all are. Throughout the entire human history, or even an entire animal kingdom, you always had the *top dog*, the one that was the strongest or the richest. Here is the silver lining; here is where it all ties together. How come a child does not act on it, and we do? This is the part where investing in yourself really makes sense. We all get greedy and we all use that greed as a fuel for certain actions. Greed in itself can never be satisfied, not in the long-term, because, by definition, greed doesn't stop when you get something, and therefore you are always longing for more. So making the choice to act on it doesn't actually make you a happier person. It only leads to more thirst in the long run, and when you eventually don't get to quench it, it eats you from the inside. So, one of the simplest ways to invest in yourself is trying to find the most honest answer to the *why?* before you make a choice. If you don't like that answer, consider a different choice. Start doing it with every major decision, and follow it through. After a while, you will see a shift in your perspective. You won't necessarily *do better* in life, but you will be at peace with yourself which you will come to realize is multitudes of times more beneficial than being miserable. Eventually, you will become a person that a 5-year-old can understand and justify, and even defend your choices.

This is at the root of my entire life philosophy. There will be times where neither choice you have available is an easy one, or the right one. That's simply the nature of life, but as long as you are completely honest with yourself and are at peace with the answer to that *why?,* these choices will eventually dwindle down. You have to invest that effort in asking the question and devote the time to try and find the answer. That's the first step.

You can use a lot of helping hands in this process. Like this book of mine, for example. I told you my life story, I spoke about the choices I made, and when you came along for the ride during that story, you lived it with me as well. You now have my experience rooted in your soul, and if a similar situation presents itself in your life, you at least have some type of a background and it will be just a tiny bit easier for you to overcome it. That's just it—you have the experience, not a thing you bought. You have a thing you lived through, that your mind and your soul went through. I am not the smartest person in the world. Heck, I am not even the smartest one in my family. I've been through so much in life, I've talked to thousands of people and experienced their problems as much as I shared mine with them. I know exactly which choices were wrong, and which were not. I perhaps didn't know it at the time, but that wasn't because I wasn't questioning them, it was simply because some mistakes in life you have to make in order to see the right choice every other time. That's also an investment in yourself and you have to embrace it, not shy away from it.

Once you master these skills of questioning your choices, of learning about yourself and others, everything else will come easier for you. You will quickly realize what you should be doing. If that entails buying the biggest house on the block, having the best car in the neighborhood, or visiting all the countries in South America and finishing your education, it will be the right choice, because the motivation behind it will be in sync with your own feelings, with your own conscience, with your own desires.

XIV. INVEST IN YOURSELF

Now, there is a specific thing that I noticed many people have the hardest time trying to figure out, and that is pride. Pride is one of the primal characteristics we are born with, and one that is the most difficult to let go of, but it is also the only motivator that has no clear malicious or beneficial side. Everything else is either beneficial or detrimental to your life. Greed is universally bad, love is universally good, etc. Pride is the weird one that is morally ambiguous and yet as strong as others, if not stronger. For example, you should easily be able to remember when your pride didn't let you apologize for being wrong, which you still regret today. You also probably have an experience where your pride didn't allow you to bow down to injustice and you acted on it. Moments like those are what your conscious is built on, and allows you to think of yourself as a good person. The point is, with pride, it is perhaps even more important to ask the question *why?* with every decision where it is involved.

There was a large portion of my life where these things, like many of us, bothered me. I could never understand it, and not until I sought the solution in prayers and religion did I figure it out. I want you to do an exercise with me right now. There is a famous story in the bible where Jesus said to his disciples.

Jesus continued: "There was a man who had two sons. The younger one said to his father, 'Father, give me my share of the estate.' So he divided his property between them.

"Not long after that, the younger son got together all he had, set off for a distant country and there squandered his wealth in wild living. After he had spent everything, there was a severe famine in that whole country, and he began to be in need. So he went and hired himself out to a citizen of that country, who sent him to his fields to feed pigs. He longed to fill his stomach with the pods that the pigs were eating, but no one gave him anything.

"When he came to his senses, he said, 'How many of my father's hired servants have food to spare, and here I am starving to death! I will set out and go back to my father and say to him: Father, I have sinned against heaven and against you. I am no longer worthy to be called your son; make me like one of your hired servants.' So he got up and went to his father.

"But while he was still a long way off, his father saw him and was filled with compassion for him; he ran to his son, threw his arms around him and kissed him.

"The son said to him, 'Father, I have sinned against heaven and against you. I am no longer worthy to be called your son.'

"But the father said to his servants, 'Quick! Bring the best robe and put it on him. Put a ring on his finger and sandals on his feet. Bring the fattened calf and kill it. Let's have a feast and celebrate. For this son of mine was dead and is alive again; he was lost and is found.' So they began to celebrate.

"Meanwhile, the older son was in the field. When he came near the house, he heard music and dancing. So he called one of the servants and asked him what was going on. 'Your brother has come,' he replied, 'and your father has killed the fattened calf because he has him back safe and sound.'

"The older brother became angry and refused to go in. So his father went out and pleaded with him. But he answered his father, 'Look! All these years I've been slaving for you and never disobeyed your orders. Yet you never gave me even a young goat so I could celebrate with my friends. But when this son of yours who has squandered your property with prostitutes comes home, you kill the fattened calf for him!'

"'My son,' the father said, 'you are always with me, and everything I *have is yours. But we had to celebrate and be glad, because this brother of yours was dead and is alive again; he was lost and is found.'"*

— Luke 15:11-32

Now take a minute to think about this story. Did you understand the point of it? Now try to use what I've talked about in this chapter and apply your logic to it. Regardless of what the Lost Son did, his father's motivation and feelings were pure. His guiding motivation was love, endless love and understanding. Was he worse off because of it? Most definitely not! Now think about the brother who stayed. His mind was clouded with injustice and with negative feelings. His envy got the better of him. Was he worse of for it? He was. Would you rather feel like the father, joyous and happy, or like the brother, envious and angry? This is where my quote makes the most sense. If the brother who stayed was a 5-year-old, would he be sad to see the Lost Son or would he be thrilled beyond imagination that his brother has returned?

> One of biggest mistakes people make in life is not living their life with purpose and passion, instead living with mediocrity and existing.
>
> — Romi Hancock

It's not easy making such investments in yourself. Compared to this, buying stuff seems a lot simpler. I am absolutely convinced that each and every one of us is capable of making such changes. Again, I am not saying that buying stuff is bad, I am saying that knowing why you want something, anything in life, is what really counts. I look at it this way. I live a comfortable life, I have a nice house, but my house is filled with books that made it possible for me to buy this house. My photo albums are filled with images that remind me of all the experiences I have lived through. Each one of them came in handy when I was making my way through the business world building a career that inevitably allowed me to have that house. Do you see where I am going with this? I constantly invested in myself and continued to do so every single day because that's what keeps me happy. I will be happy if I leave my children well situated so that they can enjoy the fruit of my labor long after I'm gone. The most important investment I have is them, and for that, I have to invest in me. Like I already said, these are strange times and whatever methods and moral values I used to raise my children may not apply for my grandchildren. So I have to stay ahead of this fast-paced society and try to shelter them while they grow up, instilling values that will allow them to explain their choices to their kids. Now you tell me, is that answer to the question *Why am I writing this book?* a good one or not? Is it applicable to your life?

Chapter 14 – Exercise

1. When is the last time you invested in yourself?

2. How did you invest?

3. What did you gain out of it?

4. Was it a good investment?

5. What is your next investment in yourself?

The best investment you can make is in yourself.
— Warren Buffet

XV. ACT AS IF YOU'VE ALREADY MADE IT

There is this word I keep coming across when reading about life, science, relationships, entertainment, etc. It is a word many of us use daily, but to be quite honest, we never think about it, and really contemplate its true meaning and the implication of its use. The word is not *love*, it's not *God*, not even *money*, which many people actually don't know the definition of; it is a word you have probably never even thought about.

That word is law.

Turn your head which way you like, and you will find law there in one form or another. The Law, governing rules and regulations of socially acceptable norms (lawyers and stuff), International Law, which not many people actually care about, but it always seems to have justification for great injustices, ironically. There are laws of physics that govern how everything works, from the smallest parts of the atom to the entire galaxy. Then there are laws of common sense like you never pee in the river upstream from your camp, etc. You can find laws everywhere, even in my corner of the world. The Law of Attraction, Law of Vibration, the Law of Cause and Effect. I came across all of these while reading up on self-help topics while discovering myself and learning about my inner thoughts and strengths. Don't get me wrong, I am not poking fun at any of these. I've learned plenty of incredible things being addressed in each of them, especially the Law of Vibration. That is something I came across years ago and it still fascinates me, and I keep finding more and more proof that there is something in it.

You might be wondering at this point, *why the hell am I talking about these laws and what is the point of it all?* Here is the thing. We are all bound by these laws, laws we invented, discovered, created, and we keep re-affirming them. So why is it that humankind as a species is so interested in these laws? I like to use a scientific definition of the word law to explain this.

Law: A statement that describes invariable relationships among phenomena under a specified set of conditions.

In simple words, a law is a rulebook that governs things and explains how they work. I've thought about this often and I came to the conclusion that we are all searching for the *Law of Life*. We all want to find out the exact rules that would guide our actions and lead us to a better life. Basically, each and every one of us, whether conscious or not, is searching for the formula that will make us happy. That's it. That is the root of our obsession. After figuring this out, I re-examined a lot of my past decisions to see how the law worked in them, the set of rules that I followed and that enabled my path to a happy life? There was no clear answer because I took a bit from here and there and made my own rulebook. I think that should be the case with everyone. The only thing you need to pay attention to is your own feelings, your own desires, and your own motivation. That's the only thing that will make sense to you and only by modeling your rulebook in accordance to those things will make it a true one.

Some of you may think that this all sounds a bit philosophical

XV. ACT AS IF YOU'VE ALREADY MADE IT

and complicated, and on the surface, you are right. Throw out the big words and you are left with a simple task of figuring out what makes you happy and how to achieve it. Simple and easy enough? Not quite. Completing your rulebook is difficult, It's a constant process that never ends because even when you do realize you are happy in life, you have to keep working at it in order to stay that way. It may sound like a hassle, but there is no greater reward.

No one, me included, can write that rulebook for you. With that being said, there are a couple of things I can help you with, things that took me years to realize, but once I finally did, they made so much sense and were clear as a day. The funny thing is that they were hiding in plain sight all along. The first thing you need to realize is that you are chasing after a feeling. No matter what you want, require, desire, lust after—it's not the real thing! You are simply chasing the feeling that thing gives you. It may sound complicated, but it's actually not.

You want a relationship because you want to be appreciated and loved. You want to have kids because you think it will make your life meaningful and provide you with a sense of purpose. You want financial wealth because you think it would make you more free and secure.

Notice that those are all feelings you seek, feelings that you think these things would provide. Do you actually need them, or could some of those feelings be triggered by something else? Let's work our way backwards. If you are seeking freedom and security, is money the only way you can achieve it? Is it, in fact, the right way? I named this chapter *Act as if You Already Made It* because that simple rule will, in fact, make you realize that the answer to the questions about money is *no*, there is more to it than just money. If you want more freedom, figure out what that word means to you and make your decisions accordingly. I figured that out before moving back to Vegas. It wasn't easy; I struggled with the thought of forfeiting most of my accomplishments. What do they actually mean if they haven't made me complete? I know now that it wasn't a risk, but rather an investment into my future. The thing that made it the right decision was that I figured out the underlying feeling I was seeking, and that was freedom. It worked out for the best because it really changed my life for the better. I left a good paying job and a bunch of clients and opted for more freedom—emotional freedom.

If you act as if you are already free, you basically become free.

If you are seeking love and appreciation, act like it. Don't get bogged down with other details, but instead nurture relationships with the people who make you feel loved and appreciated. Other people will recognize it and it will attract like-minded ones toward you, pushing away the ones who are not seeking the same. Acting like it means that you become it. There are many descriptions for this rule in all sorts of laws and philosophies. The Law of Vibration describes it as things that vibrate alike attract each other. The Law of Attraction suggests that if you are sending a certain kind of energy out into the universe, you will attract people who are sending out the same kind of energy. I really recommend you look up all of these laws and rulebooks as they are amazing, and you will learn a lot from them. In fact, after you finish this one, you should pick up any book on the subject and you will realize that each one of them has incredible insights. The more you read, and the more you learn about yourself and apply those principles to your decisions, the better your own rulebook will be.

I've read dozens of books and memorized hundreds of quotes that have helped me out whenever I lacked the motivation to do the things I dreaded doing. They all have quotes similar to *act as if you*

XV. ACT AS IF YOU'VE ALREADY MADE IT   161

already made it. Even before I came across it, I knew it to be true, even vaguely. Earlier I talked about my career as a personal trainer and a Transformation Life Coach and I outlined an exercise where I had my clients push themselves just a bit outside of their comfort zone. *Can you do 10 pushups? Try. Today you will do 4, tomorrow will be 6 perhaps. The act of trying, the acting as if you can already do 10 will eventually enable you to do them.* The same principle applies to almost anything you can imagine. I've spoken about it a great deal with a lot of people and they often tried to convince me that the principle can cause problems, like becoming delusional. *If someone acts like they can drive, when in fact they can't, and gets out on the highway, they could crash their car following your advice.* To that there is a simple reply: it's not the only rule in my rulebook as it shouldn't be the only one in yours. There is no one universal rule! If there were, this book would be one sentence long. All these chapters and pages are just a scratch on the surface of my rulebook. I just wanted you to see the big picture, the scope of it all and to try and use my experience, my guidance to compile your own formula to happiness. I have already said this: I, nor anyone else for that matter, can tell you what makes you happy. I am just here to point you in the right direction and ask the right questions. My answers to those questions may work for you, but they also may not. As long as you act like you care about them, as long as you constantly keep searching for those answers, you will keep finding them. That, you can trust me on.

Think of it this way. Imagine you were given a promise, or better yet, a guarantee that the better life is coming to you. It's not here yet, but it is coming. So tomorrow you ask: *Is it here yet?* And the answer is still no. At the end of the week you ask: *Is it here yet?* Still no, but it's just a bit closer. At the end of the month you ask: *Is it here yet?* Not quite, but if you step on this ladder, you will see it just above the hill. So the next month you step on another ladder to see it more clearly. And it is closer. And dozens of ladders later, you realize it's not beyond the hill, it is in the clouds, and every step you take, takes you closer to it. By acting on your desires to see that better life, you actually get closer to it.

You see, I just used another rule from my rulebook—Envisioning. I envisioned a scenario that helps me to better understand the problem. I turned it from a complicated matter into a simple metaphor that makes it acceptable to me. You should try the same. Many books I read call it the power of visualization and it is one of the most powerful tools a person can use as on their journey to success. I want you to think past the visualization and actually envision things. The difference is that you should only visualize about the things you are certain you want. If you envision scenarios just like I described it, you can actually figure out what exactly are you looking for and how important it is to you. It will make complicated life scenarios easier and help you better understand what the underlying feeling you are chasing is really about. I want you to consider the alternative to my rule and not act like you made it. Acting like you have already failed will cause you not to try at all, and not trying is the fastest way to fail at everything. So then, acting like you have already failed will make you a failure.

Both cycles are addictive.

If you keep acting like you have failed, you will keep failing and get into a downward spiral that will only make you more miserable. If you act as if you have already made it and keep succeeding, it will only bring you more success and keep you on that path toward the clouds, toward the better life. Luckily for the people in a downward spiral, there is a way out.

Your life, good or bad, is the result of all of your choices. If you

XV. ACT AS IF YOU'VE ALREADY MADE IT 163

don't like the result, start making different choices.

— Romi Hancock

We all make mistakes, and some, unfortunately, are irreparable. Any effort you make trying to correct your mistake is an effort worth taking, and doing so will make you realize that some mistakes you thought were irreparable actually aren't. Yes, I know the argument that, sometimes, you make all the right choices and things still don't pan out. Lifelong happiness is almost never achieved using just a single instance as a reference. In the grand scheme of things, choices are the prevailing factor.

Something else I want to talk about in this chapter is being negative. It is hard for any of us to stay positive in this world, especially with all the negative news that is constantly hitting us from every direction. I, for a very long time, thought that the world used to be a better place. After speaking with a number of historians and sociologists, it made me realize it actually isn't. There are always bad things happening around the world, but we just don't hear about them. Modern society is all about access and availability, making you present on every corner of the globe with a single click of the mouse or a swipe on your phone. Technology in itself is great, it's just the way that we use it that can sometimes be problematic—not just technology, but everything. I am not the one criticizing any ideology or teachings because most of them are actually very useful. Everything can be misused and deliberately misappropriated to justify wicked actions. Many people in the Western world these days believe Islam is a wicked religion because of so many terrorist attacks are caused by people who have been indoctrinated in that religion. That is not the case. The same could be said about Christianity because it too was used as a justification for the inquisition and prosecution of people.

If you look for negativity in things, you will easily find it.

But I would like to urge you against it. I read some of the most beautiful quotes in the Bible, and then went on to find them in the Tora and in the Quran. Different quotes explaining the same idea. Be a loving person, seek for the truth, love your neighbor. It is by looking for negativity in those beautiful teachings that you become negative as well. That only leads to anguish, to bitterness, and in the opposite direction of true happiness. So when something bad happens to you, instead of "screw you God", try looking for the consolation and understanding in prayer. As a little kid, I never understood the line: "He is in a better place now." That's what people usually say when someone close to you dies. For the longest time, I couldn't understand how a person could perish from this earth, especially a young person, and that I find consolation in that. I spoke with a pastor about it, and he told me a single sentence that made me realize it. *The more you miss them, the more you are hurting right now, the closer that person was to being happy.* It makes sense. If you miss a person after they are gone, they were a beacon of light in your life, they made the effort for you to feel loved and appreciated and they too were loved and appreciated. There is a time to mourn a person, or to mourn anything bad that happens to you. That doesn't last forever. You cannot feel sad your entire life after a tough beat like that and use it as an excuse for all of your failures. I didn't. Life was harsh on me, and I could have chosen to be negative about it, to be a failure and tell everyone I am a failure because of my childhood.

I didn't, and you shouldn't.

Don't allow bad circumstances to define you and control the rest of your life. I know it's hard, I know it may hurt tremendously. In order to overcome it and get back on that path to a happier life, you cannot afford to dwell on it.

XV. ACT AS IF YOU'VE ALREADY MADE IT

When someone asks me how the hell did I become who I am today, I usually say: I don't forget things that happened to me, good or bad. I just figure them out and make my peace with the ones I can. With the ones I cannot, I just don't let them control my future. If you tether yourself to some of those things, it's harder to climb the ladder that leads to a better life.

Chapter 15 – Exercise

1. How do you envision your life on a daily basis? Is it in a positive or negative way?

2. What feelings do you want to create?

3. Are you willing to meditate daily for 5 minutes and envision your life. I want you to focus on what your deepest desire is. What does it feel like?

What you focus on expands, and when you focus on the goodness in your life, you create more of it.

— Oprah Winfrey

XVI. LOVING THOSE WHO LOVE YOU

There was this book I remember reading when I was 12 years old. It was one of the first books I read cover to cover within a day, except this book had no covers, and some pages were missing. I never found out the title, I don't even remember the plot all that well. I remember the scene from it: a group of boys get into some kind of a battle with another group of boys and one of them gets hurt really bad. The reason this scene remained so imprinted on my mind is that it was the first time I can remember rooting for someone, from the bottom of my heart. As I was reading it, I cried my eyes out and kept hoping and praying that the boy makes it. Strangely enough, I don't even remember if he did. Every couple of years I get obsessed about finding that book, but I think some of the facts about it got mixed up in my memory and so far, I haven't been able to track it down. I think about that boy a lot, and recently I've been thinking about my obsession with the whole thing as well. Why is it that I keep remembering that book and that boy?

I don't know if my reasoning is on-point here, but my best guess is that this boy was the first person I loved without any prejudice, without ever meeting him, and above everything else, I loved him more than I loved myself. I remember thinking about it for days and imagining how if it was me standing next to him during that stupid battle, I would have fought my heart out trying to protect him. Imagining the other savage boys who hurt him would make me furious and angry and I used to imagine that I could rip them all into shreds with my bare hands. Kind of ironic, if you think about what happened to me during the following five years. That character from a random book made me realize, 30+ years later, that compassion and caring is something I have deeply rooted in every inch of my personality. I used to avoid describing myself using those words because I always figured that only other people are qualified to notice them. I used to think that you cannot possibly be objective about terms like loving, compassionate, caring, selfless, giving. I strived toward those but somehow always felt that you need other people in your life in order to achieve and to validate them. I had no friends back then. No one saw me cry and care about a fictional character from the book. To this date, I have never spoken about it. I was all those things, even as a little girl with little to none life experience. I was loving, I felt every bit of pain the boy suffered, I was furious that I couldn't help him. This all made me realize that most of us, if not all, have those traits deeply rooted in us. We are not born mean and vicious, we are created to love others and share with them, care about them, help them. So how come there are so many mean people all around us? How come these days, even kids tend to be mean and possessive? Where did all of it go wrong? Honestly, there are many partial answers to these questions, but I don't think anyone has one that precisely explains it.

I have talked to psychologists, social workers, psychiatrists, guidance counselors, parents, grandparents, and people of all sorts of backgrounds. They all have their theories as to how it happens, but none of them could really tell me why? I did notice a pattern in their reasoning, and I can sum it up in a single sentence: we got lazy.

We got lazy and complacent about the simple concept of loving the people who surround us.

XVI. LOVING THOSE WHO LOVE YOU

And part of the blame can be cast on the times we are living in. I said it before: we live in the strangest of times, and the world around us moves so fast that we fail to realize the basic principles of our nature trying to catch up with it. Let's all slow down just a bit and pause for a second.

It is so easy to devote 5 minutes a day, at the least, to the people we hold dear, give them a call, and ask them how they are feeling, how their day is going, is there something you can do to help? Prior to moving back to Vegas, I had this friend who used to leave me a voice mail every other day. She would call me at a random time to simply let me know that she's thinking about me. You know what? I always felt better after hearing her voice. No matter how hard and terrible my day was, that message would root me in place, like a thunderbolt, and all it took was 45 seconds to turn my day around. I am ashamed to admit that I wasn't as giving as she was at times.

I called her back, but not as often as I wanted. She was the one who made me realize just how powerful a minute in your day can be. I am forever grateful to her and I feel like she can take credit for half of this book being written. She doesn't even know how many times she saved my life with a simple act of love and support. I have realized it since, and I did let her know about all the stuff she did for me and how much I appreciate it, but the best way to truly honor her is to do exactly what she did: keep reminding the people around me that they are loved.

I want to tell you that I truly love you.

Even though I probably have never met you, I would like to ask you: how is your day going? Are you ok? These words I write are words of love because I care about your life. When my friends ask me, "Why would you ever want to write a book?", one of the first things that pop in my mind is, "Because I want people to read it." Sounds silly, but I really want you to read this book and feel better, feel motivated and feel loved afterwards. Hopefully, I will touch at least some of you. That's all that matters to me. I want you to read it in the same way I listened to the messages my friend left me. I want you to drop it right now, and reach out to the people you love, let them know that you think about them. There are so many terrible things going on now, we all just need a bit of love and support to make it through. I honestly believe that many of these incredibly sad things could have been prevented with a single phone call at the right time.

I recently read a story about Chen Si, a man who patrols a bridge over the Nanjing River in China. He dedicated his life to saving people from taking their own lives by simply talking to them. Angel of Nanjing, as Jordan Horowitz and Frank Ferendo described him in an award winning documentary, saved over 300 people over 15 years. Three hundred tragedies prevented with a single conversation. Three hundred families were spared the needless suffering and misery because one person had the audacity to say hello to a stranger and ask them about their day.

Why not us?

Why not you?

Are we so busy not to let our parents, kids, friends, and lovers know that we love them and that we think about them? Are we that selfish to put our loved ones on hold and keep them at a distance in order to chase shallow satisfactions? If we are, what is the point of it all? I honestly believe that these things, little signs of love and support, mean a lot more than grand gestures every other month, or a year. This chapter of the book is different than the others because I can't tell you something that you don't already know on the subject.

XVI. LOVING THOSE WHO LOVE YOU

You know this, you don't need me or anyone for that matter to explain these things to you. I wrote it anyway because I wanted you to read it:

You are loved, even though sometimes it is hard for you to see it. You are.

Pause for a minute and reflect on it. Pick a person in your life that you feel like could use your support and let them know. Now, not later, not tomorrow—now! If you care about the person, don't put it off because it will turn into a habit. A lazy habit that will only hurt you and the people you love in the long run. Don't allow yourself to become lazy. You have probably experienced this many times before: sending or receiving a drunken message from friends simply saying, "I love you, you are truly a good friend!" Do you know why that message is so frequent? Do you know why people get drunk and send it? Because alcohol strips you of the laziness and you think about people on the most primal level. It also makes you do stupid stuff as well, but you have to wonder why do you want to do them in the first place? Why do you feel the need to tell people you love them when you get drunk? It's because you feel it when you are sober as well, but you keep yourself busy with other stuff neglecting to let those people know. I want you to keep in mind that the message will always be well received, and it will always make the person on the receiving end feel better, which if you care about that person will make you feel better too.

Reach out to the person you care about. You don't have to save their life, a day is good enough. A day counts just as much. If you save them enough days, it will last them a lifetime.

— Romi Hancock

Prior to the journey of writing this book, I did a lot of soul searching, and during that period, I tried to focus on the language I wanted to use for it. For the majority of the chapters, I managed to express exactly what I wanted to, but this chapter took me a while. I was struggling to find the words to convey the importance of loving the people around us. Whatever I typed sounded forced and reminded me of the lines from soap operas, you know, the ones that make you cringe. It took me a while before I realized that this is something I had to write by hand. I sat one afternoon and started writing. All I could come up with was that quote. My original plan was to have just that quote in this entire chapter. It would have been enough to make my point, but it wouldn't be enough to satisfy my desire to reach out to all of you letting you know that you matter to me. The Nobel Prize winner Ivo Andric once said (free translation):

"We all die once, but the truly great people die twice. Once, when they disappear from the earth, and the second time when their endowment collapses."

Once I leave this earth, I want you to be my endowment. I want you, together with my children and grandchildren, to carry on and spread the love I am feeling toward you. I want to be great in that sense and if possible, never be forgotten. These words may not be the wisest or even at least important in the literary history of the world, but they will for sure be the truest. They come from the bottom of my heart and they are aimed to the same place in yours. The wording doesn't matter, and as soon as I figured that out, this chapter wrote itself. So take my advice and believe me that the wording doesn't matter. What matters is the love and the appreciation you give to the people around you. A simple statement like *I'm thinking about you* can be more effective than all the best quotes in the world.

It often is.

Chapter 16 – Exercise

1. Who do you need to call and let them know they are loved?

2. Do you feel loved?

3. What do you stand for? Does that bring up a passion in your or a calling?

If you want things to be different, perhaps the answer is to become different yourself.

— Norman Vincent Peale

XVII. BECOMING A WARRIOR

Ever since there was storytelling, we told tales about heroes, people with extraordinary abilities who did the greatest of deeds. These heroes were warriors and fighters more often than philosophers and scientists, civic leaders, politicians, etc. This is because we love the myth that people are invincible. We love these warriors because, even if it's just for a second, they give us hope that we can do something great and memorable.

My thirst for knowledge and improvement led me to many places, from seminars to lectures, books, audio and video tapes, meditation camps, etc. I've tried it all. Each one of those was a unique experience. If you open your mind and your soul, you are bound to soak up the knowledge that is floating around you. No matter how much of that knowledge and energy you take in, it's completely useless if you don't shape it, think about it, and ultimately put it to work. Having knowledge alone is pointless if it doesn't make you happy. Having money alone is pointless if you do not know what to do with it. Being famous alone means nothing if you don't have a person that understands you and that you can confide in.

Wow, did Romi just tell me that being smart, rich, and famous is a bad thing? Well, not exactly, and by the time you finish this chapter, you will have a sense of what I'm trying to convey.

*Just because you are meant to have something,
doesn't mean you are entitled to it.*

— Romi Hancock

Let me elaborate a bit on that quote. You have all heard of LeBron James and Carmelo Anthony. Do you know who Lenny Cooke is? My guess is that you don't. In 2001, Leonard Cooke was ranked higher than both of those players. He was regarded as the best basketball talent since Michael Jordan. He was meant to be great, even beyond great, and he thought he was entitled to success.

That was his mistake.

While all the rest of his classmates and opponents were up at 6:00 am running drills and attending practices, he was asleep. Additionally, he slacked off in school and soon became ineligible to play for a high school team. His woes continued as no college would take him on. He never got to play in the NBA and never achieved the greatness that he was "destined" to. Entitlement is the thing that you earn, that you live up to. That's the beauty of it. Entitlement literally means the fact of having a right to something. It is you alone who shapes the sense of what you have rights to. The thing is, feeling that you deserve something and that you are meant to have comes second to the living up to it part. Living up to it is where the grit and grind come into play and where you really forge your warrior mentality. Understanding and accepting that is what separates happy and unhappy people.

The person standing between you and your life goals is <u>you</u>. Most of us can relate to Lenny because we all felt like failures at some point in our lives. I am fairly certain that those feelings come from the desire to achieve or attain something tainted by the lack of careful planning and resolve to grind it out. That's where we are pitted against ourselves. Lenny had the precision, the speed, the vision. The rest of the guys had the resolve and the grit to improve.

They worked on it.

They worked on their shot until it became automatic, deeply embedded in their muscle memory. They worked on getting faster by competing with themselves, constantly looking to beat the time set yesterday. When they failed, they didn't quit; in fact, quite the opposite.

I want you to imagine a warrior. What does that look like for you? Who is that person for you? What makes them special? Is it an ancient gladiator in the arena fighting a couple of lions? Is it a samurai dressed in full body armor fighting off 6 foes at a time? A single mom working 2 jobs to support her children? For many of you, these images will be true. Those are good examples, granted. I've got others that come to mind. A warrior I see is a person who comes home after working their butt off, makes an effort to spend quality time with their family, and devotes that smidgen of free time they have to make their lives better. My warrior is a fireman that trains every day, tirelessly, just so that they can make it to save one more person. My warrior is a Medical student doing a residency and pulling 36-hour shifts fully aware that there may come a time where the difference between someone living and dying comes down to them making the right decision despite the stress and fatigue.

It's not contentment that makes you a warrior, it's overcoming adversity to become one.

— Romi Hancock

True warriors are not born, they are not mythical characters that you read about in the books who never lost a fight and place honor above everything. I don't believe in that. A true warrior has experienced defeats and victories alike. I've seen it so many times—a "warrior" suffers a single defeat and fails to come back from it, finding excuses why they failed short and justification for their defeat. They are not afraid of failing, they are afraid of falling from grace in front of their audience.

> *A victory only introduces you to the world. You gain so little from it. The defeat, on the other hand, is what introduces the world to you. And you get a whole world from it.*
>
> — Romi Hancock

Wow, did Romi just tell me that being a failure is actually a good thing? Again, no. I went to the extremes in both cases in order to show you that being super-successful, super-rich is not all there is to experience in life. Similarly, being broke and constantly failing is not the worst thing in life. I am saying that the audience matters. The motivation matters. You matter, because in both cases, if you are succeeding and failing for the wrong reasons, it won't make you happy. Previous chapters spoke about finding your purpose and creating a roadmap for achieving it. This chapter is all about staying on that path and not giving up. My idea of a warrior is a person that knows what needs to be done and tries their hardest to take care of it. Once you become such a person, once you have a clear vision, your belief in what you are doing, you need the resolve and perseverance to keep pushing toward it. When you do end up failing, people around you, the people you love and respect, do not see you as a failure. They admire your effort and they love you even more for it. It is their reaction that will fuel your desire to try again, and again, and again. It is their wisdom that will show you the way around the mountain if they see it as insurmountable. A true warrior is not deaf to the advice that comes from the hearth. This is what you need to become in order to be truly happy. Success alone will not do it, even if it makes you happy for a little while. Defeat alone does not matter if you do not learn from it and grow from it.

I used to think I was stubborn as hell. When people told me something couldn't be done, I was ready to break my back just to prove them wrong. That was the case for almost my entire life, or so I thought it was, but writing this book made me question a lot about my life, and my stubbornness was one of those things. The more I thought about some of my decisions and actions, the more I realized that many of the things I did weren't motivated by it. I didn't finish my education because I was told it couldn't be done. I finished it because I wanted a better life for me and my kids. I simply knew that I had it in me to power through, but failing to complete that wouldn't make me a failure because I knew that I had it in me. I failed my real estate exam the first time I took it, and it didn't define me. It wasn't the stubbornness that made me take it again, it was my resolve to pursue that career. Once I finally succeeded, and it felt great for a long time. It still feels great; it wasn't shallow, which means that my inner warrior was empowered by it. I have tried writing a book a couple of times, each time falling short. I did not get discouraged because I knew I had it in me. For me, this is what it means to be a warrior. Pursuing the things you feel will make you and the people around you happy, people you care about.

If there is an obstacle blocking your path, find a way to overcome it.

Don't give up because it will make you doubt yourself. Instead, expect to fail sometimes and in fact, plan for it. You have to make sacrifices and you will suffer defeats along the way, but as long as you learn from your mistakes and you stay true to yourself, it will be easy for you to start again. Becoming a warrior means knowing quite well that you may suffer another defeat this time, and still be willing to try. True warriors are humble in victory and hopeful in defeat.

When I spoke to people about what's going to be in this book, many of them asked me why I want to tell the whole world of the suffering I endured as a child. This is something I came to terms with a long time ago. Everything that has happened to me made me the person who I am today. It was horrible, and I wouldn't wish it on anyone, but I am not ashamed of my life, and I am not defined by the negative things that have happened to me. We witnessed so many confessions and reports of abuse that have happened over the last couple of decades. I truly believe that talking about it is the first step to embracing it. My message to all of you who have suffered any kind of abuse is: Don't stay silent and suffer, speak up, bring it into the light and deal with it. The only thing I want you to pay attention to is the reason why you are doing it. If you have some kind of trauma that lingers above your head, you should make your peace with it.

Do not label yourself as a victim.

I am not a victim. I am a survivor that used all the experience in life, good and bad, for empowerment. My past experiences, my suffering, my happiness, the in-betweens. It's all fueling my resolve to keep pushing forward and keep molding my inner warrior.

Speaking up about horrible experiences is pointless if you are looking for a spotlight. It's not about seeking an audience that shows compassion, that's not the warrior's way. For me, speaking up is about empowerment and proving to yourself that bad experiences do not define you, that you are strong enough to overcome them and use them to learn about yourself and become a better person despite what you have endured. I know what true pain feels like, and naturally I don't look forward to it; but I am not petrified of it either. If these things that hurt me have to happen in order for me to learn the lessons I am destined to, I am ready for them. The way I see it can be explained with a simple example. Every woman is a warrior.

XVII. BECOMING A WARRIOR

The act of childbirth is painful, and yet no woman shies away from delivering a child. It is an experience no man could ever go through, but a lot of women do. No matter how hard it is, no matter how much it hurts, you don't ever talk about it with shame or hide it from others. You wear it like a badge on your armor: you survived giving birth, it was hard, but from it you gained so much—a whole world in fact.

I want you to remember that no matter what happened to you, there is a person inside you that can come to terms with it. That person is strong enough to cope with the consequences, to draw lessons even from the mindless acts of pure madness. That person is your inner warrior. If you let it speak up, let it figure out how to move on, it will carry you forward. That warrior has the strength, the resolve, the endurance to carry you through the rough times. If you keep silencing it, if you hide it and don't allow it to make peace with all that's bothering you, you will struggle. You become a victim, not a survivor, and that can be a defense mechanism—for a while. If it hurts too much for you to speak about it, don't force it. Take it slow. Ask for help. A true warrior will always offer a helping hand, so it's only natural for them to accept it when they need it. There is always a way back, even when you have lost all hope. That's why we always like to root for the underdog because, at some point in our lives, we all felt like one.

Lenny is a motivational speaker and a basketball coach these days. For a while there, he was a victim of his own mistakes. He grew from it and learned the lessons he was destined to. In my eyes, he is now a bigger person than he ever would have been as a basketball player. He now uses his story to empower the young minds, to empower his own warrior, and to keep going forward having full knowledge of what he has lost.

He came to terms with it, and so did I, and so will you.

I will hear from you again, you will speak up about it, and you will overcome your hardships and let your inner warrior grow. If and when it becomes too hard, too painful, hopeless, stop, and look for a helping hand. You will find it, or at least, you will find me. Don't ever forget that there is always a way back; you may not see it at the moment, but if you don't give up, you will find it!

We all have such tremendous power hidden deep within us and we are all capable of achieving greatness. Although we are not all created the same, true greatness is attainable by all of us. For some that greatness means fame, power, wealth, prosperity, being a role model for our kids, etc. For others, it may just be rediscovering how to be an honest father, a loving mother, a loyal lover, a righteous brother, a gracious sister.

A warrior.

*You have to experience painful pressure in life
to achieve anything worthy.*

— Romi Hancock

Chapter 17 – Exercise

1. Are you ready to become the warrior of your life?

2. What are three non-negotiables that you MUST complete in this lifetime?

3. Are you ready to start the journey of creating the life you imagine?

4. Are you ready to become the wife, husband, friend, sister, son that you would want?

Ultimately you are in charge of the destiny you hold.

— Romi Hancock

XVIII. CREATE A ROADMAP AND FOLLOW THE STEPS

Life is a strange, and we can only hope that for most of us, it's not a time spent in vain, filled with regret and contempt. I do believe that many people, myself included, at least at some point in their lives would wish for the hardships to end and for things to get easier. It's just a natural feeling and sort of a defense mechanism for all of us. Many of us will spend many years of our lives still hurt by the mistakes and the pain suffered. Don't run from that time, but embrace it and use it to figure out who you are, what are you made of, and do your true priorities lie.

Don't focus on the bad things you had no control over.

It's not going to do you any good and it will press on you like a massive cross that would prove too difficult to bear the further you go with it. Simply let it go and try and look for ways to assume the responsibility for the things that went wrong while you are in control. Look for reasons and closure rather than for excuses and self-pity. That's the hardship you need constantly in your life. Owning up to your mistakes and learning from them, moving on by improving, adapting, and coming out the other side a better person—that's the slow progress you need to start valuing.

The thing about incremental progress, and in general taking responsibility, is that most people go about it the wrong way. I've seen countless examples of this. During my personal coaching days, there was a pattern that kept repeating with several of my clients. Most people decide one day they want to lose weight. They go on a diet, start working out, buy a scale and weighing themselves every morning. I'm going to guess that some of you did the same many, many, many times and for some, it worked, but for most, it took somewhere between a week and a couple of months before giving up and go back to stagnation. I can tell you with absolute certainty that I know at least three to five reasons for this. First of all, weight loss and fat loss are two completely different things, but many people fail to even consider that. When you decide to get into shape, you have to figure out exactly what it is that you are trying to change. If you have extra fat, it's probably because of the stress of your work, you sit a lot, can't commit to healthy eating because it's expensive and time-consuming, etc. None of these things is out of your control. Own up to it. If you have extra body mass, not fat but you are simply big, the muscles are there you just don't have the time or the energy to work out and get them toned. Again, well within your control. Or maybe you are just big-boned. Do I even need to say it?

If you recognize any of these, here is a good place to start. Let go of the thing that doesn't serve you—those are the excuses. It's always the first step in any transformation and even though it's a small one, you have to make it on your own. This works for any transformation, whether it's physical, emotional, professional, you name it and it applies. So, now that you have figured out exactly what it is, you need to figure out how to change it. I'll stick with getting back into the desired shape for this one because it's so obvious but no one seems to realize it. Getting back into shape is not just about losing weight and getting slimmer or leaner. It's the state of your whole organism, body,

XVIII. CREATE A ROADMAP AND FOLLOW THE STEPS

and mind alike. Figure out an outlining goal and divide the journey into smaller chapters. Let's say you want to lose 20 pounds. Start by figuring out your strengths. You don't mind working out but are terrible with diets? No problem, don't go on a diet, don't lower your food income, just structure it better. That's a start. Don't eat when you are not hungry, don't eat because you are bored, don't eat just before bed. Eat every meal at approximately the same time. Instead of 3 really big meals, divide the same amount of food into 5 or 6 portions and ration them throughout the day.

Not a big change right? But trust me, it is scientifically been proven that this method alone will help you reduce your weight. Notice the phrasing there, help you reduce, not MAKE YOU LOSE weight. So you took care of that for a month, while focusing on your workouts. The scale shows the same. Disappointment, almost a fear-like sensation rises, "I can't do it". Let go of that fear because it's not real. The results are false. Even though you may not lose any weight during that first month, you will feel better, more energized, and more confident that you made at least a small positive change in your life regardless of the results. Give it another month, and then another. Keep repeating the same process, constantly adjusting, and making small improvements. One month you cut down on your dinner, the next one you add more healthy food to your daily routine, and so on. Make your meals 80% like you want them and 20% healthy. You will figure out that healthy food is neither expensive nor disgusting. Perhaps the next month you move that to 70/30. After a couple of months, you get to the reversed state, 80% healthy and 20% not. It's only normal that you crave certain foods you really like and now are bad for you, but so what? Indulge yourself once in a while. Check your results in 3 months, in 6 months, a year. See if you fail to make any progress then.

This is the struggle I was referring to. That little type of hardship produces real and long-lasting achievements and results, the type you feel really good about every single day, not just temporarily. You could have liposuction, get rid of 20 pounds of fat in a day, and then what? How long do you think that good feeling will last? How long before you put the weight back on? Fast solutions are not the key to long-term success in life.

Figure out your goal and draw out a roadmap on how to get it, break it down into smaller steps and start following it. This applies to your relationships as well. Perhaps you are not happy with the personal, family, or business relationships in your life. We've all been there at some point, and more likely than not, we will again. Own up to it and take the first step toward mending those relationships. Do you want better communication with your family? Make an effort. Go out on a limb and try to improve that what you don't like. Do you want to expand your social circle? Put yourself in positions to meet new people, take that first step, and once you figure out exactly what you want, go after it. If you are attracted to someone and really want to take that relationship to a higher level, go for it. Don't wait for fate to come knocking on your door and do the work for you. Yes, inevitably, you will make mistakes. Don't linger on it, forgive yourself. Most people after a bad breakup don't have a problem with the person who hurt them, but rather with themselves, for letting it happen. If you don't agree, consider this: when a person hurts you, you have a difficult time opening up again for a while, right? If the person who hurt you is no longer part of the equation, why are you hesitant? It's because the problem is within you. You are angry at yourself for letting someone hurt you. Don't be. Embrace it and forgive yourself. The sadness can only last until you find happiness, but the anger doesn't subside until you forgive. Trust your instincts and let them guide you through relationships. If you are true to yourself, your in-

XVIII. CREATE A ROADMAP AND FOLLOW THE STEPS

stincts will never fail you. This seems hard and unattainable at times; but again, small steps make this path easier. In every relationship, try to find your purpose, your role, and keep asking yourself, *do you like it? Is that me?* If the answer is *no* more often than *yes*, then it's time to go back to step one and let go of what doesn't serve you, and go through the roadmap again.

Hopefully, you get to the point where you have found yourself, and the answers to the questions about your life are more positive than negative. You shouldn't stop there and become complacent. Challenge yourself to keep making those small improvements. You might find it contradictory that I am advising you to keep working hard even when you are mostly happy about your life. That's not contradictory at all, but consequently. If you are at a point where you feel happy about the majority of your life, it's probably because you worked to get there. You know that life has a funny and cruel way of surprising you with an occasional shit-show, to pardon my language. If you don't continue working hard at it, these shit-show events will gradually move that needle back to the negative side of the scale. You know what? Sometimes, even when you work really hard, that happens anyway. Your life gets turned inside out without any apparent reason and that's where the anger, sadness, and most of all, anxiety kicks in. Attack it head on, don't hide, don't suppress it. It's your life and it's worth fighting for it with every atom of your strength. Your life is a war, and these events that I mentioned are only battles. A single battle can rarely win a war. It's a certainty that it will win it if you give up after you fail. I already told you all the reasons why failing is great, but I want to remind you again. Every failure is the way life tells you that you know where you want to go; you just need to pick a different path.

Most failures in life are only street signs that guide you towards the real destination and move you away from the pitfalls leading to the abyss.

— Romi Hancock

When you find yourself in such a pit, it's only the end of the world if you stay there. That means you do not desire more out of life, and that you've made peace with being miserable. That's contradictory right there. You can't make peace with being miserable, because making peace with something means accepting it in a positive way. There's nothing positive about being miserable and staying that way for the rest of your life. Use whatever knowledge you have at your disposal, whatever tools you need in order to pick yourself up. I'm not talking about taking advantage of the people or situations. I'm talking about applying those tools to yourself to start with—make peace with yourself. Forgive yourself for the mistakes you made but don't linger on the past of drawing conclusions where you went wrong. Instead of spending all that energy and effort on angst and despair, invest in yourself and be the positive change in the situation, in people, in life. There is one thing I keep repeating to myself whenever I get bogged down by my mistakes—lead by example. You've made mistakes, but don't wait for others to show you how to rebound. Let them help, especially if their motives are pure, but no one can do the work for you.

Nothing in life brings out character like adversity. Your true power lies in how you take on situations, events, and people when the odds are stacked against you. This is how warriors are made.

If at first you don't make it, act like you did.

Not in a way that you lie to people and yourself, but in a way that makes you realize your limits. You may have not yet reached your goals, but you are a warrior for even trying. You know why? Because too many people are too scared to even try. When two boxers compete for a title, two people step into the ring, and two warriors step out. Granted, one of them is a champion, but a true warrior is great in wins and defeats alike. So act like you are a champion and you will become one. Love those around you the same way whether you are at the top of the world or at the bottom, and in all spaces in-between. Do it honestly and without prejudice because you want only the same treatment from them. A true warrior is always loved by their people, and they love their people just the same. That's why a warrior is willing to do anything for them. Being a warrior is not an achievement, it is a calling, and a life-long one at that.

People are so afraid of dying that they're afraid of living.

Romi Hancock

Chapter 18 – Exercise

1. I want you to do a five minute inner meditation and I want you to ask yourself these questions:
    a. How will it feel if I do not go after my deepest desires?
    b. What is the worst thing that can happen by NOT doing it?
    c. What is the worst thing that can happen by DOING it?
4. Map out your biggest obstacle and create a map on how you can navigate away from it, and then navigate toward what you truly want.

5. Are you willing to do the work in order to achieve your own greatness?

6. What are three things you will start right now to achieve your deepest desires?
    a.
    b.
    c.

4. Can you commit to starting to exercise? 15 minutes a day this week and in two weeks work up to 30 minutes, if need be?

5. Are you willing to start loving yourself more by feeding your body what it really needs?

In order to become your most inspired, powerful and true self, you must first decide to be just that.

— Romi Hancock

CONCLUSION

I want you to know that I believe in you. You were not just born to exist and you reading this book is proof of that. God would not put that hunger in your heart if He did not have a purpose for you. You are not too old or too young to start. No excuses!

I have given you the worst that went on in my life; and not to say that I didn't have more very difficult challenges or that I didn't slip back into what was once my "normal", but the point is that I persevered and I did not stop. I had my share of challenges and failures, but I DECIDED that I wanted more.

Lifestyle changes are never easy, but neither is dying from bad choices, physically, emotionally and spiritually.

— Romi Hancock

Whether you think you can ,or you think you cant't, your right.
— Henry Ford

PRINCIPLES TO PURSING AND CREATING PASSION, WEALTH, AND HEALTH

1. Letting go of what does not serve you and creating what does.

2. Finding your strength; it's in there.

3. Letting go of the fear that holds you back, attack it and win.

4. Taking the first few steps will cause a ball rolling downhill effect.

5. Going after what you want, deciding to do it, and following through.

6. Forgiving yourself, allowing yourself to have had failures and letting them be your greatest lessons.

7. Trusting your instincts; yes, that gut feeling is right, learn to trust it.

8. Finding your purpose, learning to figure out why you were born.

9. Challenging yourself, pushing yourself to the next level.

10. Attacking anxiety. Stop lying to yourself just to live life in the safe zone; life in general is not safe and playing there will not bring out your greatness.

11. Failing is great, failing is fundamental. Let it guide you, not stop you. You did not fail 100 times, you simply found 100 ways how not to do it.

12. Desiring more out of life. What happened to your desires and dreams? It's still in you, it just needs to be reawakened.

13. Using the knowledge around you. Success leaves clues and there are proven recipes to help you to accomplish your dreams.

14. Invest in yourself. Just like feeding your body, you must feed the mind.

15. Act as if you have already made it, using the techniques of visualization to manifest.

16. Loving those who love you, not caving in but showing strong, pure love.

17. Becoming a warrior. It takes work, and you must do what it takes.

18. Following the steps in the roadmap laid before you to create a mindset that ultimately brings you success with your passions, wealth, and health.